THE ACCESS TUTOR

THE ACCESS TUTOR

Dolores laGuardia
University of San Francisco

Hans P. Guth
Santa Clara University

Allyn and Bacon

Boston ▪ London ▪ Toronto ▪ Sydney ▪ Tokyo ▪ Singapore

Vice President: Eben W. Ludlow
Editorial Assistant: Grace Trudo
Executive Marketing Manager: Lisa Kimball
Text Design and Electronic Composition: Peggy Cabot, Cabot Computer Services
Composition Buyer: Linda Cox
Manufacturing Buyer: Suzanne Lareau
Cover Administrator: Linda Knowles

Library of Congress Cataloging-in-Publication Data

laGuardia, Dolores.
    The access tutor / Dolores laGuardia, Hans P. Guth.
        p.   cm.
    Includes index.
    ISBN 0–205–28621–6 (alk. paper)
    1. English language—Textbooks for foreign speakers.   2. English
language—Rhetoric—Handbooks, manuals, etc.   3. Report writing—
Handbooks, manuals, etc.   I. Guth, Hans Paul.   II. Title.

PE1128.L29 1999
808'.042—dc21
                                                                99-051328
                                                                CIP

Text Credits: page 9, "Six Bay Area Women Chosen as Finalists," *San Francisco
Chronicle,* February 24, 1999. © The San Francisco Chronicle. Reprinted with per-
mission. **page 10,** "Pirates of the Cyberbucks," by John Carman, *San Francisco
Chronicle,* June 18, 1999. © The San Francisco Chronicle. Reprinted with permis-
sion. **pages 10–11,** "U.S. Economy Robust," by Martin Crutsinger. © Associated
Press. Reprinted by permission. **page 11,** "Interview with Sonia Sanchez," by Annie
Finch, in *The Writer's Chronicle,* March/April 1999. Reprinted by permission of the
author. **page 12,** "Latina Magazine Finds Its Niche," by Eileen Glanton. © Associ-
ated Press. Reprinted by permission. **pages 45–46,** "Who Goes to College?" by
Jimmy Breslin from his commencement address to CUNY graduates, June 7, 1999.
Reprinted by permission of the author. **pages 57–58,** "Harnessing Brain Waves," by
Dale O'Reilly. First appeared in *The San Francisco Examiner,* June 27, 1999. Reprinted
by permission.

Printed in the United States of America

10 9 8 7 6 5 4 3 2 1   04 03 02 01 00

CONTENTS

WORDS

SENTENCES

Contents

MECHANICS

ESL ESSENTIALS

Contents

PREFACE

The Access Tutor is more than a routine workbook. It provides reinforcement of essential terms and concepts as well as habit-building practice.

1   *The Access Tutor* is a teaching text with special emphasis on motivating and engaging students who may have had disappointing experiences with English in the past:

- It maintains a positive supportive tone in helping students extend their range and in building their confidence in writing standard English.
- It provides a mix of traditional and nontraditional exercises and activities.
- It makes traditional English teachers' terms accessible and functional for students with varying preparation.
- It employs a distinctive teaching pattern with headings like CAPSULE RULE—BACKUP EXPLANATION—PROBLEM SPOTTER—INSTANT REVIEW—EDITING PRACTICE.
- It provides varied interactive review and rewrite activities instead of monotonous right-or-wrong exercises.

2   *The Access Tutor* is tailored for a variety of teaching needs:

- It is consumable—with tear-out worksheets for peer review, prewriting, quick-check quizzes, and revision and editing practice.
- It is ideal as a supplement for courses with students who have been mainstreamed in the name of phasing out "remedial" or developmental courses.
- It is ideal for use in writing centers or by writing tutors.

3   *The Access Tutor* offers special help to teachers reaching out to nontraditional students:

- It helps students make the transition from local or social varieties of nonstandard speech to standard written English.
- It provides explanations throughout that are accessible to ESL students, with a special final section on writing English as a second language and learning English as a second culture.

4   *The Access Tutor* is cross-referenced to serve as backup, reinforcement, and additional habit-building practice for laGuardia and Guth's *The Access Handbook*. However, it may also be used as a stand-alone text for students needing additional preparation or support for college-level writing. An *Answer Key* is available from the publisher.

In developing the materials in this book, we have owed a special debt to colleagues dedicated to offering a second chance to students whose previous education had failed to meet their needs. We owe thanks to the many students we have taught and learned from over the years, whose intelligence, idealism, and aspirations give the lie to the condescension visited upon them by elitist pundits and time-serving politicians.

THE ACCESS TUTOR

A   MOBILIZING YOUR RESOURCES

What are your assets as a writer? What do you bring to a writing class? What will help you improve your writing?

1   **You have the gift of language.**   Everyone's brain is wired to produce words and sentences to express every shade of meaning. Your job in a writing class is to activate more of your language potential. Make better and fuller use of it.

2   **You have instant access to information.**   To find answers to your questions, you can go to the Internet. You can get material from the book shelves of your library. You can also go to a newsstand offering every kind of newspaper and magazine. You can talk to others, bouncing ideas off your classmates or friends. Your job is to plug into the resources of information and opinion that are everywhere around you.

3   **You have the right to make your voice heard.**   This country has a long history of honoring free speech. Most Americans believe the most important right is to say what they think. You have the right to your own opinion. All you are going to be asked is to explain and support what you have to say. How do you know what you know? Why do you think what you think?

4   **You can trust the power of the good example**.   Make sure you learn from how things are done right. Learn from models of good writing. Take time to appreciate words well used, sentences well written, or points effectively made. Pay special attention to the work of professionals and fellow students who do things well. Ask what went right before you ask what went wrong.

5   **You can get feedback and support.**   Everyone is sensitive to criticism. However, for writers to learn from feedback is a way of life. Pay special attention to readers who show you how to build on what you do well. At the same time, try to learn from reviewers even when their reactions seem negative. What bothered them? What do they need to have explained? If they disagree with you, what can you say to change their minds?

6   **You have the chance to revise and improve your work.**   In a world of deadlines, it's a privilege to have time to research a topic. It's a privilege to have a chance to revise and rethink an early draft. Make use of opportunities to fill in missing evidence or to answer objections. Take time to work in second thoughts.

7   **You will interact with people from different backgrounds.**   You will have a chance to branch out—to go beyond ideas familiar to you from your family, friends, town, or group. Learn from encountering different ways of looking at the same thing. Become more aware of the range of people who might be part of your audience in a multicultural society.

B   INTERACTING WITH OTHERS

In a writing program, you play a double role: You are both writer and reader. You are both author and audience.

■ As a writer, you learn from **instructor feedback.** You look for clues to what you did well and what needs work. You learn from the reactions of other students in **peer review.** You look for positive advice that is the golden mean between just friendly encouragement and just fault-finding criticism.

■ In turn, as a reader, you serve as a **trial audience** for other writers. You think about why you reacted positively or negatively about a piece of writing. You begin to read with the writer's eye. You ask: Why is this effective, or why is this weak? What would I have done differently?

You and your fellow students may want to use or adapt a peer review sheet like that on the next page. For instance, you may use it in small groups when you rotate drafts or finished papers for peer response. Or you may use it as a template—a ready-made form to fill in—when you exchange papers by e-mail or other means. As your turn comes to read another student's paper, answer questions like the ones on the sample response sheet.

Date _____

Writer _____   Reader _____

Title _____

1   What did the writer want to accomplish? What was the writer's purpose or agenda? What made the writer want to write?

_____

_____

_____

_____

_____

2   How would you sum up the main point of the paper? Is it clearly stated as a thesis or central idea? Where?

_____

_____

_____

_____

_____

3   Does the paper have a clear plan? Does it move forward in purposeful fashion? Can you outline several major stages or several major steps?

_____

_____

_____

_____

_____

4   How well does the writer support his or her opinions? Are there strong, convincing examples? Did you notice any striking quotations or testimony from insiders or witnesses? Did the writer use facts and figures to support key points?

_____

_____

_____

_____

_____

_____

5 Was anything exceptionally well explained? Or did anthing puzzle or confuse you? Does anything need more follow-up or explanation?

_____

_____

_____

_____

_____

6 What kind of reader would be the ideal audience for this paper? Are you? Why or why not?

_____

_____

_____

_____

_____

7 Do you have any special personal questions for the author? Do you have any special personal reaction?

_____

_____

_____

_____

_____

_____

_____

_____

_____

CAPSULE RULE   Develop a personal interest in your topic.

Writers write effectively when they care about the topic. (If you don't care about your topic, how could the reader?) Some writers have a strong personal interest in an area of work or field of study—for example, computers, child care, or women's studies. Some have a special personal connection with topics like prejudice or abuse. Others are on a mission: They plead with you to support a cause, or they sound a warning about bad news. For example, they may plead with you to help save the forests. They may ask you to support the development of new technologies to help people who are disabled.

YOUR INTEREST INVENTORY

What would you include in a **personal interest inventory?** Do you get excited about topics in the news? Do you get angry about things that happen at school? Are you a fan of celebrities? Do you admire some political leaders and dislike others? Do you support causes? List briefly four or five topics that could get you excited.

_____

_____

_____

_____

_____

List briefly four or five topics that are likely to bore you.

_____

_____

_____

_____

_____

FOLLOW-UP A

Participate in a **ranking** of possible writing topics. For instance, do you get excited about anything in the *world of sports?* In July 1999, the final games of the Women's World Cup of soccer created tremendous enthusiasm. Over 70,000 fans watched the semifinals in Stanford Stadium, and over 90,000 fans watched the final between the U.S. and China in the California heat at the Rose Bowl in Pasadena. As one columnist said, "zillions" more (including millions in China who had stayed up till the early morning hours) watched the final shootout of penalty kicks (5–4 for the U.S.).

Rank the following possible topics on a scale from 5 (best) to 1 (worst):

a Can you get excited about events like the final in the Women's World Cup? Why or why not?

b Do you think young women should be encouraged to be athletes rather than cheerleaders?

c Some fans claim that baseball is the most American sport. Others claim it's football. Do you want to take sides?

d Some sportswriters claim that superstars earning millions from advertising contracts make everyone lose sight of the true meaning of sports. Do you agree or disagree?

e Some critics claim that Americans are obsessed with sports and neglect the true cultural achievements of the nation—for instance, in the fine arts, in music, or in the theater. Are they right?

RANKING: 5_____ 4_____ 3_____ 2_____ 1_____

WRITING OPTION

Write on the topic you ranked highest. Use the space below to prepare a **journal entry** on the topic. In your journal, you can put down questions, ideas, and examples in a more informal fashion than in a full-length paper. Often, a journal entry can serve as a first run-through for a paper in which your ideas are more fully developed and sorted out.

_____

_____

_____

_____

_____

_____

_____

_____

_____

_____

_____

_____

_____

_____

_____

Name _____

FOLLOW-UP B

Participate in another **ranking** of possible writing topics. Young Americans are often accused of apathy—not really caring about what is happening to their country. In a recent national election, the percentage of young people voting in the lowest age bracket was down to 25 percent.

Rank the following possible topics on a scale from 5 (best) to 1 (worst):

a Does the low turnout among young voters mean that for young Americans democracy is dead?

b Are there any political leaders that you would consider role models?

c Do you care about the environment?

d Do you think Republicans and Democrats are really different?

e Is feminism a thing of the past for today's young women?

RANKING: 5_____   4_____   3_____   2_____   1_____

WRITING OPTION

Write on the topic you ranked highest. Use the space below to prepare a **journal entry** on the topic.

_____

_____

_____

_____

_____

_____

_____

_____

_____

_____

_____

_____

_____

_____

CAPSULE RULE   **Size up the background, interests, and needs of your audience.**

Writers ask themselves: Who is listening? Who is my audience? Will anything I say make a dent? (Why or why not?) Some writers appeal mainly to an **in-group audience** sharing their interests or commitments. For instance, a writer discussing strained relations between a community and the police may address mainly readers who side with law enforcement personnel and their families. Another writer may appeal mainly to readers who object to police abuses in the treatment of minorities. Finally, some writers aim at a more **general audience.** They try to find common ground and ask their readers to listen to the other side.

WRITING THE AUDIENCE PROFILE

Study the following excerpts. Can you tell what kind of audience the writer had in mind? Prepare an **audience profile.** Answer questions like the following:

- Who would be the ideal audience for this selection?
- What are some of the things that would matter—age group, gender, occupation or career interests, social class, and ethnic or racial group?
- What kind of background might the reader need?
- Would the audience be a small limited group, or could it be a larger possible audience?
- Do you personally make a good audience for this selection? Why or why not?
- Who would be the wrong kind of reader (or maybe the worst possible audience) for this selection?

1   **6 Bay Area Women Chosen as Finalists**

Six Bay Area women are among approximately 85 finalists in the first national Entrepreneurial Excellence contest sponsored by *Working Woman* magazine.

The local finalists include Laura Scher, CEO of Working Assets Funding Service; Sabrina Horn, CFO and president of the Horn Group; and Michelle Burke, CEO of Executive Counterparts.

The other Bay Area finalists are Jennifer Maxwell, co-founder and owner of PowerBar Inc. in Berkeley; Fran Lent, president of Fran's Healthy Helpings in Burlingame; and Eleanor Mason Ramsey, president of Mason Tillman Associates in Oakland.

Working Woman magazine will choose national winners from its pool of finalists in April.

—*San Francisco Chronicle,* Staff Report

_____

_____

_____

_____

_____

_____

_____

_____

_____

_____

_____

2   Pirates of the Cyberbucks

"Pirates of Silicon Valley," the film starring Noah Wyle as the founder of Apple Computers, isn't as funny or barbed as its creators seem to think it is. But it's still one of TNT's more ambitious efforts, and it's never less than entertaining.

It's surprisingly tough on its star marauders, too, especially Jobs, the visionary who founded Apple Computer with Steve Wozniak (Joey Slotnick). Wyle is easily the film's strongest presence as a charismatic figure with an almost mystical belief in what he and computers can accomplish. "This ain't just business," Jobs declares. "This is practically spiritual. This is about overthrowing dead culture." By now he's screaming at employees, bullying job applicants and even alienating Wozniak.

On to Gates. Hall seems more intimidated by the thought of playing the world's wealthiest man. His performance is stilted and lacks the fluidity of Wyle's, though it never crashes all the way to robotic impersonation. The Microsoft founder is depicted as a struggling wannabe who lives on pizza and bluff, who speaks the language of money as well as the language of computer operating systems, and who swipes the keys to Windows from Jobs' Macintosh prototype.

—John Carman

_____

_____

_____

_____

_____

_____

_____

_____

_____

_____

3   U.S. Economy Robust

WASHINGTON—Federal Reserve Chairman Alan Greenspan said yesterday that a "surprisingly robust" U.S. economy should continue growing this year but at a much slower pace than last. And he dropped hints that if the slowdown doesn't occur, the central bank is prepared to increase interest rates to make it happen.

Greenspan called the economy's growth rate in the fourth quarter "torrid." He also repeated worries he expressed last month about whether the stock market's return to record levels is justified in the light of the weakness in corporate earnings. Some economists say Fed rate increases could occur as soon as May if the economy doesn't slow.

The U.S. economy grew at a sizzling 5.6 percent annual rate in the final three months of last year, pushing the unemployment rate down to the lowest levels in three decades. The central bank has seen no evidence yet that the tight labor market has caused inflationary pressures, Greenspan told the Senate Banking Committee, but the growing shortage of available workers "constitutes a critical upside risk to the inflation outlook."

—Martin Crutsinger

---

4   **Interview with Sonia Sanchez**

I wrote about my stepmother, who was a Southern black woman and afraid of New York. She couldn't find something that she needed on 125th Street, so she asked us to take her downtown to Macy's, which was a store for all people. It wasn't Best & Co., it wasn't Lord and Taylor, it wasn't Saks Fifth Avenue, it wasn't any of those other stores that perhaps if you went in as an African-American they would follow you around the store forever.

So Pat and I took her there, and she found what she wanted, and she brought it to the counter. But she just stood there, because she knew her place, my stepmother did. And I remember looking and thinking to myself that my stepmother was fearful of this confrontation. And the saleswoman wouldn't touch her hand or anything, and wouldn't say, "Here you go." I saw all that as a child, and understood it as a child, and was thinking to myself, "I'll never let any one do that to me."

—Annie Finch

_____

_____

_____

_____

_____

_____

_____

_____

_____

5   **Latina Magazine Finds Its Niche**

NEW YORK—After a string of successful sales calls with America's major automakers, Christy Haubegger was flying high. Still clad in her gray pinstriped suit and high heeled shoes, she bounded down the hallway of her hotel. Looking forward to a cool drink and a warm bath, Haubegger recounted, she filled her ice bucket and headed back to her room. An older couple spotted her, and asked, "Dear, will you be bringing ice to all the rooms?" Haubegger, the founder and publisher of _Latina_ magazine, had been mistaken for a maid. Her perfect day last spring ended with the thought that even in her business attire a stranger saw her youthful face, tiny frame, and brown skin and assumed she was an employee, not a guest, at the $150-a-night Detroit hotel.

A desire to change perceptions like those helped motivate Haubegger to launch _Latina_ in June 1996. The magazine shares newsstand space with a growing number of publications targeting the Spanish speaking market, but it is the only truly bilingual magazine, with stories in English, shorter summaries in Spanish and Spanish slang interspersed throughout.

—Eileen Glanton

_____

_____

_____

_____

_____

_____

_____

_____

_____

_____

_____

CAPSULE RULE Explore your subject before you write your paper.

Students sometimes complain that they don't have enough material for a paper. Professional writers often have the opposite problem. They often collect more material than they can use. They have stacks of material hard to sift and fit into a limited space. To make sure your writing does not seem thin or weak, follow basic advice for working up material for your papers:

1 Explore a full **range of sources.** Suppose you want to write about poverty in our affluent society. Where would you turn for material?

- First, draw on your own **experience.** Did you ever see poverty from close by? Did you ever see poor people, food stamps, people wearing secondhand clothes, or people lining up in front of a soup kitchen?
- Second, draw on current **observation** and investigation. Where or when do you see poor people now? Do you see people begging for small change? What do their signs say? Can you talk to someone on welfare?
- Third, draw on current **media coverage.** Do newspapers and news programs pay attention to the poor—or only to the rich and famous? Do politicians ever go to the ghetto or the barrio? When they do, what do they say or do?

2 Move in for a **closer look.** Narrow your focus. Change is a keynote of our fast-moving society, but it is also a vast topic. A student writer may decide to take a close look at one actual ongoing change: changing career opportunities for women. He starts with personal observation of women working as lawyers or doctors. He discusses the career choices of his mother and older sister. He draws on an interview with a woman working as an engineer. He draws on statistics in *Newsweek* concerning women in construction, police work, and management.

PROBLEM SPOTTER

Passages like the following are a warning sign that the writers are not using their own eyes and ears. They are not beginning to use the resources available to writers from their own experience, their reading, the media, and the Internet:

SECONDHAND GENERALITIES: "We live in a complex, fast-moving world. We live in a changing world that we were not trained for. Much of what we are taught is already out of date. We should not look backward but forward."

PUFFING UP THE SUBJECT: "The homeless question is a very important issue in our society. We all need to give serious thought to this important social question. It deserves a place high on our national agenda." (Show us *where* you personally see this issue and *why* it is important)

DICTIONARY DEFINITIONS THAT SAY NOTHING NEW: "*Webster's* dictionary defines *justice* as the practice of being just and fair."

TRITE SAYINGS: "There is a silver lining to every cloud." "It takes all kinds."

MOBILIZING YOUR RESOURCES

Among the following topics, choose one for which you can work up material from a range of sources: new immigrants integrating into American society, rude or hostile public behavior, computers in the schools, student attitudes toward the police, fear of crime, vulgarity in programs for the young. For your chosen topic, prepare brief notes under each of the following three headings. Print out your notes for feedback from your instructor or peers.

1 Sketch out two or three incidents or *observations* relevant to your topic.
2 List one or two people you could question or *interview:* insiders, experts, witnesses, people in authority. Explain briefly their credentials or possible input.
3 Identify briefly articles, TV programs, movies, or books you could draw on. What material might they provide?

USING PREWRITING TECHNIQUES

Learn to draw on the full range of possible sources of material. Do a trial run of two gathering techniques. Print out the results for feedback from your instructor or your peers.

1 Do a sample **brainstorming**. Call to mind whatever you know or remember on a topic like the following: diet fads, the exercise fad, the macho mystique, dropouts, relationships, advertising techniques. Here is a possible model (on advertising techniques or advertisers' ploys):

headache tablet: "wipe your headache away"
car turns into a panther
the dream family: smiling parents, clean-cut kids, a dog
car has control panel like a spaceship
apply now: "nobody can be turned away"
insurance for veterans: wave the flag
truck bounces through rugged country
oven cleaner: "wipe it off"
fun crowd on beach: no-calorie drink
mouthwash attracts handsome young man
lumberjack beer drinkers—the great outdoors

2 Try using a **discovery frame**. Use a set of questions that systematically explore a topic:

1 What striking example, incident, or statistic could bring the issue into focus?
2 Where and how is the issue covered in the media—in newspaper or newsmagazine articles, TV, movies?
3 What role has the issue played in your personal experience—in your growing up, in your family, with relatives, or in school?
4 What can you learn from current investigation—observing current trends, talking to insiders?
5 What can you use from previous reading or study—books, coursework, textbooks?

3 Prepare a set of questions for **interviewing** an insider or person in the know. Here is a possible model (on police work):

How does one become a police officer?
Why did you decide to become one?
What is the daily routine like on the job?
What is life like for a police officer's family?
What do you think about the portrayal of the police in the media?
What movie or TV program does the best job of giving a true picture?
How do you react to charges of harassment or police brutality?
What do you think helps or hinders you most in your job?

Name _____

Study the use of material in the following student paper. Study the way it starts from personal experience, moves on to observation of friends, and then relates the topic to a larger national pattern as seen in media coverage. What material does the writer use under each heading?

From the WRITING OPTIONS that follow the paper, choose a topic that you could develop in a similar three-step pattern.

The Right Move

Mobility: The word has come to mean something that a hundred years ago was unimaginable. We no longer simply move from one house to another as the family needs more room. Today, moves from city to city, from state to state, or from coast to coast are common. Are we losing something as a result of this ability to pack our possessions into a truck, wave goodbye to our neighbors, and leave our "sweet home"? I don't think so. The wonderful thing about our modern ability to move is that we can search out that location where we fit in or where we can be content.

(material from personal experience:)

I grew up in a small town in Michigan; the population was 1,000 people. The only Americans I knew were white middle-class farmers. Because I had friends out West and jobs were scarce in Michigan, I decided to move to Los Angeles at age eighteen. I carried a jar of pickled watermelon rind and some homemade strawberry preserves in my suitcase. At the airport, as I hugged my parents goodbye, I had to force myself to believe that I had made the right decision. However, no amount of college could have taught me as well how diversified America is as my move across the country. In my hometown there was only one black family. I had never met Filipinos, Mexicans, or Japanese. Today I work and go to school with people from many different backgrounds.

(material from firsthand observation:)

Several of my friends have gone through the experience of making the right move. When I was still in high school, an older friend's parents announced that they were moving to the East Coast. My friend was reluctant. She had planned to stay in her hometown, raise a family, and farm like everyone else. But she finally sold her horse, threw away her overalls, and headed east. She is now one of the few from our town with a college degree and a different career. However, finding contentment does not always mean moving away from the farm. Another friend of mine had grown up in Los Angeles but had always dreamed of fishing, hiking, and raising children in a quiet country atmosphere. He moved to a tiny town in Iowa where, as he puts it, "even the mayor is unemployed." He is doing carpentry jobs to help support his family and is happier than ever before.

(material from reading:)

A recent survey in *Better Homes and Gardens* found that four out of five people who had moved from one state to another were originally reluctant when the decision was first made. Three months after those moves, though, nearly all of them had positive feelings about the move and thought it a change for the better. People from farming towns in Michigan, steel towns in Pennsylvania, and fishing towns in Maine are discovering that moving can be a revitalizing experience.

WRITING OPTIONS

Collect material for a paper that explores the same three dimensions: firsthand personal experience—firsthand observation of others close to you—material from your reading or viewing. From the following list, choose a topic that you could take through these three major steps.

- alienated or hostile kids
- the return of big gas-guzzling vehicles
- the triumph of junk food
- the growth of women's sports
- gurus or personal trainers and handlers
- diet fads
- _____ (a similar topic of your choice)

Use the space below for some brainstorming or other preliminary note-taking on the topic.

CAPSULE RULE Push toward a thesis—try to sum up your main point.

Early in your paper, make a statement that sums up the main point. What is your paper as a whole trying to say? What is the message that you want your reader to remember? Zero in on a key issue. Answer a key question. Sum up your central idea as the **thesis** of your paper. Here is an example:

> THESIS: **The evening news gives us a distorted picture of American life.**
> (Typical fare:
> child molesting at pre-school
> enraged suitor kills young woman
> drunk driver kills three
> liver transplant fails)

BACKUP EXPLANATION

Tell your readers early in your paper what the main point or key idea of your paper is. Weak papers often range all over the map. They may touch on several interesting points, but they don't zero in on them and drive them home. Do the following to strengthen your papers:

- Try to sum up your central idea, or **thesis**, in a single sentence. What is your paper as a whole trying to show or to prove?
- State your thesis early in your paper—often at the end of a short **introduction** that brings the topic to life.
- Spend the rest of the paper presenting the examples, details, or reasons that show what you mean. (If you made a general point, what does it mean in practice? If you summed up a trend or a process, how does it work? If you made a claim, what is the evidence?)
- Try making your thesis a **preview** of the organization of the paper. Let your readers know what to expect.

> THESIS: **The many relatives and big family occasions of the old-style family are rapidly becoming a thing of the past.** (We expect first some nostalgia scenes from the past and then *contrasting* pictures of the present.)
> THESIS: **Diets vary greatly: crash diets that promise spectacular results, diets using supplements to suppress appetite, and long-range balanced diets for those who care about their health.** (We expect full treatment of each of the *three major kinds* in turn.)

PROBLEM SPOTTER

A student writes about the visibility of immigrants in current American life. She gives her readers some snapshots of immigrants she encounters:

- a hard-working Vietnamese family runs a corner grocery
- immigrants working as tellers in a local bank have language problems
- neighbors make remarks about women from Iran wearing the traditional head covering

Readers will ask: "What is the point? What are you trying to tell us? What are you trying to prove?" The following paper has a point—the writer is raising a key issue or answering a central question. The paper has a central idea, or thesis.

A Meeting of Cultures

THESIS: **Hostility toward immigrants is often caused by our failure to understand cultural differences.**

- Filipino women don't like to be told to be "friendly tellers" and smile at customers of the local bank. (They don't want to seem to be "loose women.")
- Other Asian employees don't nod or say "I see" when managers talk to them. (The polite thing in their country was to listen silently and attentively.)
- Iranian women wear the traditional head covering because they had religious training teaching them it was immodest to show their hair in public.

INSTANT REVIEW

A **trial thesis** is a first tentative attempt to sum up the unifying idea of your paper. For each paper-in-progress, choose the most promising trial thesis. Circle the letter of the best trial thesis:

PAPER 1: A Japanese American friend hates to be asked "What are you?" Black students hate to be typed as different just because of the color of their skin. Many students are allergic to "kidding" references to the shape of their eyes or to their accents. . . .

    A We no longer hear much about "hyphenated Americans."
    B Young people hate to be typed as different because of surface traits.
    C People should try to learn English and become like everyone else.

PAPER 2: When the computer is down, airlines cannot book flights. When a computer error occurs in our checking account, correcting it takes the patience of a saint. When a copilot punches the wrong data into a flight computer, people may die. . . .

    A Everywhere we turn, we run into computers.
    B Some people love computers; others hate them.
    C We are increasingly at the mercy of the computers that do our work and our thinking for us.

REVISION PRACTICE

In each of the following pairs, one possible thesis is weak. It does not make a strong point, or it tells the reader nothing new. The other choice is a promising thesis—it makes a central point that the rest of the paper could support. Circle the letter of your choice for a stronger thesis. For several of these, write a few sentences justifying your choice.

1   **a** America's colleges offer many different kinds of opportunities.
     b Colleges today try to help those who have been denied educational opportunities in the past.

2   **a** The homeless are an embarrassment, so we try to hide them from view.
     b In many of our communities, we see homeless people in the streets.

3   **a** We live in a modern age of fast-moving change.
     b Young women are taking aim at many professions that were once dominated by men.

4   **a** We see Japanese products everywhere in our society.
     b The secret of Japanese-made cars was pride in quality and rigid quality control.

5   **a** The cost of current medical advances is staggering.
     b Modern medicine is advancing by leaps and bounds.

_____

_____

_____

Name _____

PREWRITING PRACTICE

Each of the following statements is a possible thesis for a short paper. Choose three of the pairs. For each of these pairs, select the version of the thesis that comes closest to your own view. Then sketch out possible material you might use to support the thesis. List possible details, examples, reasons, or arguments. Write your choice of thesis and your sample materials for your instructor or for discussion with your fellow students.

1 Women should (should not bother to) learn the art of self-defense.
2 "Buying American" will (will not) help save jobs in America.
3 Peer pressure is (is not) the major cause of drug abuse.
4 Americans are becoming aware of (paranoid about) the health hazards in their food.
5 Current crime shows glorify (do not really glorify) police officers who bend the law.

_____

_____

_____

_____

_____

_____

_____

_____

_____

_____

_____

_____

_____

_____

_____

_____

_____

_____

_____

_____

CAPSULE RULE Lay out your material in a pattern that the reader can follow.

Lay out your material in a pattern that makes sense to the reader. Use a **working outline** or a trial outline to map out your tentative plan. Sketch out major parts or major stages of your paper. Then adjust your working outline as necessary as you go along. Use basic organizing strategies like the following. Or adapt them for your own purposes:

1 **TIME SEQUENCE** Readers can easily follow a pattern that goes from past history to present trends. They can easily follow a contrast of **then and now.** They can also easily follow a pattern that looks at current trends and projects them into the future.

2 **PROBLEM SOLVING** When you identify a problem, your readers are prepared to look for possible **causes.** They are primed to look at one or more possible **solutions.** They are ready to ask: What brought this on? And what could have been done differently?

3 **THE LARGER PICTURE** Readers can easily follow a progression from the **private to the public.** For example, they will be able to follow a two-step pattern: What role has an issue played in your own individual experience? How has the issue affected a larger circle of friends and family?

4 **THE CLOSER LOOK** Readers can follow a pattern that goes from superficial impressions or a **stereotype** to taking a closer look. They can follow as you check out the truth behind a popular negative stereotype about an ethnic or racial group. They can follow along as you examine the reality behind advertising slogans.

BACKUP EXPLANATION

Writers often give their readers a **preview** of their overall plan. They give at least a strong hint at the beginning of how a paper is laid out. Readers get discouraged when they can't find their bearings. They need answers to questions like the following:

- What is the plan? What is the program? Where are we headed?
- What are the major stages in this process, or what are the major steps in your argument?
- Why is this in here? How does this fit into your overall plan?

PROBLEM SPOTTER

A paper on prison reform may register miscellaneous grievances. For instance, one single toilet was available for inmates in a large holding cell. Prisoners were penalized for communicating their grievances to the press. Is there any overall pattern to tie such grievances together? The student writer needs to lay out the material in a pattern that the reader can follow:

Cruel and Unusual Punishment

I Substandard facilities—overcrowded cells, primitive sanitary facilities, tasteless starchy food

II Substandard health care—sick prisoners treated as malingerers, suicides by untreated mentally ill patients

III Silencing of prisoners—difficulty of contacts with supporters, denial of access to the media

INSTANT REVIEW

Study the following **working outlines** and discuss them with fellow students. How clear is each outline? What details or examples does it make you expect?

1   **Growing Up with Sports**

   I FIRST STAGE: The outsider—watching others play
  II SECOND STAGE: The team player—joining in
 III THIRD STAGE: Working out for personal development

2   **Second Chances**

   I Childhood memories of a happy family life
  II Personal memory of an early marriage and divorce
 III Trying to make a second marriage work

3   **Traffic Gridlock**

Possible solutions:
   I Encouraging car pools
  II Special lanes for car pools and buses
 III Flextime or staggered working hours
 IV Better bus transportation
  V Light rail

REVISION PRACTICE

The following are possible subheadings for student papers. Choose one of these lists that could be better organized. For instance, rearrange the first in the best **chronological** order, or order in time. Or reorder the second in reverse **order of importance**, going from the least promising to the most promising. Share your rearranged sequence for feedback.

Women in Sports

women gymnasts prominent in recent Olympics
tennis and ice skating as first popular women's sports
football and baseball still mainly male domains
female tennis superstars
no women in original Greek Olympics
women prominent in today's running craze
growing interest in women's volleyball and basketball teams

Staying in School

free tuition
help from family or relatives
low-cost government loans
part-time work
winning in the lottery
establishing residence if an out-of-state student

_____

_____

_____

_____

_____

Name _____

PREWRITING PRACTICE

1   The following sample outline shows a classic pattern of *growing up*. For each of the three stages, fill in one or two examples or details from your own experience or from your observation of others. Be prepared to share your material for feedback from your instructor or peers.

FIRST STAGE: Uncritical acceptance of parents' authority

_____

_____

_____

_____

_____

_____

SECOND STAGE: Teenage resistance or rebellion

_____

_____

_____

_____

_____

_____

THIRD STAGE: Striking out on one's own

_____

_____

_____

_____

_____

_____

_____

2   The following sample outline sorts out some possible suggested solutions to the problem of *growing divorce rates*. For each of the solutions, fill in some possible details. Or provide comments based on your own experience or observation. Be prepared for feedback from your instructor or peers.

FIRST SOLUTION: Lowering expectations—expecting less than a perfect romantic experience or a perfect mate

_____

_____

_____

_____

_____

_____

SECOND SOLUTION: Discussing career choices and economic prospects fully before marriage

_____

_____

_____

_____

_____

_____

THIRD SOLUTION: Equal sharing of chores and responsibilities in marriage

_____

_____

_____

_____

_____

_____

_____

CAPSULE RULE Study feedback to learn how you can improve your writing.

How much time will you have for revising and rethinking? Each paper is different. However, teachers and editors again and again recommend basic ways of strengthening your writing. Look for two kinds of comments especially:

- What are you doing well? (Keep doing it.)
- What needs work? (What can you do to strengthen an early draft?)

If time permits, instructors may give you **feedback** like the following:

1 POINTED TITLE
"You need to go beyond weak generic titles like 'Health Care.' What about health care? What's going to be your point? Try a title that suggests a point of view or an agenda—for instance 'High-Tech Medicine?' or 'Our Sick Health Care System' or 'No Time to Be Sick.'"

2 LIVE INTRODUCTION
"You need to bring the issue to life more—*dramatize* the issue. You say that the media are obsessed with celebrities. How about starting with a dramatic example—such as days and days of media coverage when the son of President Kennedy was lost in his small plane at sea?"

3 THESIS AS PREVIEW
"Make your thesis an actual statement. Go beyond saying that there are 'frequently asked questions' or that there is 'much controversy concerning this topic.' *What* questions? Use your thesis to give a strong hint of what's *ahead* in your paper."

4 STREAMLINED PLAN
"You need to *highlight* the three or four major parts of your paper more. Signal a major turning point here as you turn from the problems of inner-city schools to alienated kids in the suburbs. (Avoid weak links like *also* or *another*.)"

5 STRONGER SUPPORT
"It's time to move in for a closer look here. This key point needs stronger support. Give several related examples. If you can, fill in data or statistics."

6 STRENGTHENED ATTRIBUTION
"Who said this and where? Give author and source (so this does not just sound like hearsay). If you can, summarize briefly the credentials of key sources to show that they are authorities or insiders."

7 STRONGER CONCLUSION
"Try not to retreat into saying that 'everyone is entitled to an opinion' or that 'time will tell.' If you can, end with positive concrete suggestions for action. Or look for a strong final example or clincher quote."

QUESTIONS FOR SELF-CRITICISM

A Do any of the sample comments above apply to one of your own papers? Do any of them help you pinpoint something that is also an issue in your own writing? Explain how or why.

_____

_____

_____

_____

_____

B What comments or instructor's feedback have helped you most with your own writing? What was the problem? What did you learn?

_____

_____

_____

_____

_____

_____

_____

_____

_____

_____

C What comments or feedback on your writing bothered you or left you confused? What was the problem or the issue? What help do you think you need with it?

_____

_____

_____

_____

_____

_____

_____

_____

_____

_____

Name _____

Study the **before-and-after** versions of the following writing samples. On a separate sheet, provide before-and-after versions of examples from your own writing for several of these basic revision strategies.

1   **POINTED TITLE**—Rewrite your title to make it show more of your attitude or agenda.
    BEFORE: The Female Standard of Beauty
    AFTER: **Fitting the Mold**
    Fighting the Beauty Myth
    The Unattainable Ideal

2   **STRONG OPENING**—Rewrite a weak general introduction that does not bring the subject to life.
    BEFORE: The media today endlessly reinforce the image of the ideal woman. Young women are constantly bombarded with the pictures of models and stars that live up to the image created by the media. . . .
    AFTER: **Slim long legs, pancake-like stomach, tiny waist, and a large chest—this is the image of the ideal young woman that American women today see over and over again on the covers of *Vogue, Glamour, Elle,* and the lowliest biker magazine. . . .**

3   **TAKING A STAND**—Early in your paper, spell out more clearly what your paper as a whole is really trying to show or to prove (your thesis).
    BEFORE: A question arises how much the younger generation is interested in politics. Many seem to be bored with electoral campaigns and show little interest in candidates of either party. . . .
    AFTER: **In a recent national election, fewer than 25 percent of the youngest eligible group of voters went to the polls. If this is a general trend, democracy has no future.**

4   **PROVIDING STRONGER SIGNPOSTS**—Include early a strong hint or *preview* of your overall plan, and signal major *transitions* or turns in the road.
    BEFORE: Americans value attractive appearance, as we can see from the media. This applies not just to women but also to good-looking men. . . .
    AFTER: **Americans value attractive appearance in both sexes more than character or achievement. Attractive females are seen as more feminine than others, but attractive males are also seen as more masculine. Attractive women and men both are both viewed as smarter, more interesting, more poised, and more successful than others. . . .**
    The juvenile fixation of the media on stereotyped female beauty is easy to document. . . .
    It is less often pointed out that the tall handsome distinguished-looking candidate or the one with the boyish fraternity look has the advantage over the bespectacled Woody Allen lookalike. . . .
    Only in recent years have the media recognized strong self-reliant women who do not look like waifs and who are at ease in their bodies. . . .

5   **SUPPORTING YOUR POINTS WITH EXAMPLES**—Feed in strong detailed examples (authentic real-life examples and not made-up or hypothetical ones).
    BEFORE: Violence itself is nothing new and has been around since the earliest times. What is new is that we are accepting it as a major source of entertainment. . . .

AFTER: Young Americans have become used to a steady diet of violence that gets more brutal each year. Young people became increasingly desensitized as the hockey-masked maniac in a succession of *Friday the 13th* movies hacked apart scores of teenagers in the most brutal fashion. Video games have since moved on to scenes of unimaginable brutality. In games with names like *Mortal Combat,* the loser may have his spine removed, his body split down the middle, or his body cremated on screen. . . .

6 **SUPPORTING YOUR POINTS WITH QUOTATIONS**—Quote authorities or insiders who agree with you.

BEFORE: The United States has a long and deep-seated history of guns since the early colonial days. Many articles and editorials discuss the issue of the ever-presence of guns in our society. . . .

AFTER: America from colonial days has carried on its love affair with the gun. A columnist in the *Washington Post* says in an article titled "Congress under the Guns" that "handgun shootings are a bloody way of life across America.". . .

7 **SUPPORTING YOUR POINTS WITH STATISTICS**—Feed in detailed facts and figures to get beyond hearsay and vague impressions.

BEFORE: The face of American medicine is changing. Women are entering medical school in large numbers. . . .

AFTER: The face of American medicine is changing. By the early 1990s, for the first time women made up 50 percent of the students accepted in medical schools around the country. According to Jill Waalen, writing in the *Journal of the American Medical Association,* by 1997 women represented 43 percent of medical students who actually enrolled. . . .

8 **ACKNOWLEDGING VIEWS ON THE OTHER SIDE**—Don't just ridicule the opposition but address key concerns.

BEFORE: Shutting down logging operations to save the spotted owl is too absurd. . . .

AFTER: It is true that the habitat of our remaining wildlife is steadily shrinking. However, settlers and farmers have always moved in on the wilderness to serve human needs. . . .

9 **PUTTING YOUR THINKING IN YOUR OWN WORDS**—Don't fall back on familiar sayings or clichés.

BEFORE: Those opposing affirmative action have concluded that two wrongs don't make a right and enough is enough.

AFTER: Those opposing affirmative action have concluded that the injustices of the past cannot be made good by new injustices and that at some point we all must make our way on our own.

10 **ENDING ON A STRONG NOTE**—Conclude with a strong reminder or concrete suggestions for progress.

BEFORE: The media are dangerous because they have the ability to affect our images of ourselves and affect our minds drastically. We need more realistic and less unhealthy images of what women are like. . . .

AFTER: Women must go through the long journey of working to appreciate who they are as human beings. They must stop comparing their bodies to those of the stressed-out, lettuce-eating "top models" exploited by a male establishment. In the words of Naomi Wolf, "Ideal beauty is ideal because it does not exist."

Writing is an interaction between writer and reader. In a writing program using a workshop format, you may often be asked to review other students' writing. There may be opportunities for sorting out the reactions of *different* readers to the same piece of writing.

What can you do in your peer reviews to help make writing a positive experience for yourself and your fellow writers? Keep basic points in mind:

- *Every writer hopes for a receptive reader.* See if you can say: "I see what you are trying to do." Make an effort to see what the writer was trying to do before you evaluate how well the writer did the job.

- *Try to do justice to the writer's effort as a whole.* Try not to pass over most of what the paper says because some statement made you angry or seemed ignorant to you. (Try not to "go off on a tangent.")

- *Writers look for concrete suggestions for improvement.* The question in the writer's mind is: "How can I do better?" Make specific recommendations for up-to-date examples to use. Recommend a recent article you remember reading. If something was offensive, suggest a better way of wording what the writer was trying to say.

- *Target major needs.* Much important criticism gets lost when it is buried among minor points. Don't scatter your fire. What is most important for the writer to think about and to remember?

Finally, remember that writers write for their own satisfaction as well as for an audience. Some of the best writing is done by authors who can say to themselves: "This is something I wanted to check out. I learned something from this paper. I did an honest job. If others also learn something from this paper, or if I change anyone's mind, that's great. But first I have to satisfy myself."

Your instructor may ask you to write a response to a paper *as a whole*. Or the instructor may provide a set of *suggested questions* for peer review. Here are some examples:

QUESTIONS FOR PEER REVIEW

1 **PURPOSE**—How would you sum up what the writer focused on or set out to do?

2 **THESIS**—What is the writer's thesis? Where is it stated? How would you restate it in your own words? Does it set up a program or pattern for the paper to follow?

3 **ORGANIZATION**—What is the overall plan? Does it make sense? What are the major sections or stages of the paper? Are they easy or hard to follow?

4 **SUPPORT**—Is there enough support for the author's opinions or conclusions? Are there good examples, quotable quotes, or detailed statistics?

5 **STYLE**—Was the writing clear? Was anything confusing? Was the writing lively? Do any images stay in your mind?

6 **BEGINNINGS AND ENDINGS**—Were title, introduction, and conclusion effective?

7 **READER RESPONSE**—Did you learn something from this paper? Did it change your mind? Did it confirm what you knew or believed? Did you enjoy reading the paper?

QUESTIONS FOR PEER REVIEW—CURRENT ISSUES PAPER

1 How does the writer bring the issue into focus or bring it to life?

2 Is there a thesis or initial overview that clues you in to the overall agenda of the paper?

3 Where does the writer turn for supporting material? Does it seem reliable, informative, or convincing?

4 How well does the writer handle questions or objections? Has the writer listened to "the other side"? Do both sides seem to get a fair hearing?

5 Has the writer tried to reach a balanced conclusion?

6 Do you personally learn something here about the topic? Does the writer make you think? Does the paper change your mind or make you rethink your own position on the topic?

WORKSHEET 8A   **A Paper for Peer Review**

Name _____

Don't Cry for Feminism: It's Still Alive

Is the feminist movement really alive? A short time ago as I sat in my English class I began to doubt seriously the validity of this statement. When neither I nor any of my peers would even consider this subject as a topic for a paper, the issue of feminism appeared irrelevant and unimportant. However, the need for equality is neither irrelevant nor unimportant. There must be a problem when you consider that today men are ten times more likely to get a management job, eight times more likely to get a raise while working at that job, and likely to earn almost two times as much in that same job as a woman would.

Many people are unclear on who qualifies as a feminist. When I asked students on campus who they thought would be a feminist, I received answers that were very ignorant and stereotypical. Most people described a feminist as an outspoken, short-haired, portly, man-hating lesbian. However, studies done by the Feminist Majority Foundation, the largest foundation of its kind, have found that 57% of all women are self-proclaimed feminists. This statement not only proves the stereotype false, it also shows how a new stage of feminism in our society appears to have reached an ample audience. The FMF defines feminism in more detail by calling it "the policy, practice, or advocacy of political, economic, and social equality for women. A feminist is any person—woman or man, girl or boy—who advocates feminism." The goal of the feminist movement is not to present women as victims, to bash males, or to be angry. Its sole purpose is equality.

Women have not yet reached equality. The number of women firefighters, police officers, construction workers, college presidents, and corporate heads has increased substantially in the last two decades. Nevertheless, as reported by the Commerce Department Census Bureau in *Current Population Reports,* "Women still comprise only 3% of firefighters, 8% of state and local police officers, 1.9% of construction workers, 11.8% of college presidents, and 3–5% of the senior level jobs in major companies."

Even though it may not have been easy for me to recognize at first, I realize now that feminism is needed to improve the position of women in many aspects of daily life. As a former high school athlete, I recognize that my opportunity to play sports was a product of Title IX, the law passed in the 1970s which guaranteed the same opportunities to female athletes as it did to males. Laws such as Title IX were fought for by feminists in order to gain equality for young women such as myself, without which I may not have been given the opportunity. Although I was given the opportunity to play, women are still discriminated against in athletics. As the Office of Civil Rights in the Department of Education reports, "Most schools and colleges are in violation of the law; equal distribution of money, scholarships, and playing opportunities just is not happening."

As I sit in a classroom today I must wonder if I am not somehow counted as less than the male students sitting next to me. I must also consider that in three years, after having graduated from college and faced with looking for a job, I will once again be subjected to this trend of gender inequality. I made the mistake of dismissing feminism as something that was unimportant to me, dismissing it as something for other women. Harriot Stanton Blatch, daughter of the lifelong suffrage leader Elizabeth Cady Stanton, stated: "Their struggle for the ballot took over 70 years of constant, determined campaigning, yet it did not take a single life, and its success has endured. . . . Without firing a shot, throwing a rock, or issuing a personal threat, women won for themselves rights for which men have launched violent revolutions."

PEER REVIEW 1: The writer discusses how the feminist issue, and inequality directed toward women, is still a major issue, although many have dismissed it. Her points seem very convincing that this is still a major issue but has in a sense been forgotten.

The *thesis* or point of the paper is quite clear: Feminism should still be considered today and inequality toward women is still occurring. The statistics presented, especially the ones about women and jobs, strongly support her thesis.

About the *audience:* Is she just talking to women or to men also? I am not sure she should call the people she interviewed "ignorant" even though some probably are.

The findings in this paper showed me that inequality is still a major problem. I guess I can be considered one of those who dismissed it as a problem; however, I was wrong, as the paper shows.

PEER REVIEW 2: In the opening paragraph, you give figures and *statistics*—give a source for these? The Title IX paragraph could be stronger if more support and stuff were incorporated. This is strong support for the paper.

The *conclusion* is good. This is a strong part of the paper. Very strong "clincher quotation."

I can easily see where you stand on the issue. You give good examples and statistics. Maybe you could incorporate ideas like positions for secretaries still posting for attractive females. With a little work, this could be a kick-butt feminist paper.

PEER REVIEW 3: (YOUR TURN—Your reaction here)

_____

_____

_____

_____

_____

_____

_____

_____

_____

_____

_____

_____

_____

_____

_____

_____

CAPSULE RULE Get your readers' attention and leave them with a strong impression at the end.

As a writer, your basic job is to bring together relevant information or useful evidence on your subject and to make sense of it. You sort it out, laying it out to show how everything fits together. However, once the main body of your paper is in rough shape, you are likely to ask:

- Is anybody listening?
- Am I taking my readers with me?
- What will it take for my message to reach my readers?
- Will they remember what I was really trying to say?

You then pay special attention to the following:

TITLE How do I compete with other claims on the reader's attention? What title will tell my readers what my subject is—but at the same time promise them something that will be worth their time?

INTRODUCTION How will my readers see what this is all about? What striking incident, example, or quotation can bring the subject to life?

THESIS Early in the paper, do I clearly spell out for my readers what I am really trying to say?

TRANSITION Am I taking my readers with me from one point to the next? Do I provide the signals that will help the reader follow?

CONCLUSION What can I do to provide a strong sendoff for my paper? What striking example or quotation can I save for the last?

INSTANT REVIEW

1 Look at the following *beginning and ending* of a student paper. Answer questions like the following:

- What makes the **title** inviting or intriguing?
- How does the **introduction** bring the subject to life? In what direction does it point the reader?
- How well does the introduction lead up to the **thesis?**
- How does the **conclusion** wrap up the discussion? Do you think it makes the reader feel that the paper led somewhere—instead of just running out of steam?

TITLE: **Vandalism: Footsteps in the Night**

INTRODUCTION: Under the cover of darkness, teenagers cover freshly painted walls with obscene graffiti or with scrolls blossoming in various colors of spray paint. Vandals do their work at night. The owner of a new car walks out to the car in the morning only to discover that someone has taken a key and etched a thick line in the paint, from the back fender clear to the front of the car.

THESIS: **To me, vandals are people who take out their rage by secretly doing damage to someone else's property. . . .**

(main body of the paper here)

CONCLUSION: How do we minimize vandalism? In my high school we had a big concrete wall that was used for single tennis, and it was common to have the entire wall painted with student garble. When it was so full that nothing could be added, the school would hire someone to white it all out. But of course within a week the wall was filling up again. During my last year the principal set up a program to have the artists in the school paint a mural on the wall. All students had the opportunity to submit suggestions for the painting, and everyone had a chance to vote for the end result. Four years later, as I drive by, the wall remains covered by student art rather than by obscene messages from the stalker in the night.

_____

_____

_____

_____

2 How does each of the following *beginnings* get the reader into the topic?

The Police—Your Friend and Helper?

A friend of mine walks down East 14th Street after being with friends in a predominantly minority neighborhood. He sees some police officers arguing with a neighbor and stops to ask one of the officers what the problem is. He is told to mind his own business. Believing that what happens in his neighborhood is his business, he repeats the question. An argument ensues. Suddenly, without warning, the officer punches the concerned citizen who is subsequently maced and thrown in the patrol car. He winds up in a cell by the booking desk. There is a big difference between reading about the police in the newspaper and seeing them in action at first hand.

_____

_____

_____

_____

It Comes Down to Values

Everyone is learning not to feel guilty about greed. An executive who paid himself over twenty million a year wrote a best-selling book telling others how to do likewise and sold over six million copies. In cities that can't afford to pay teachers a living wage, quarterbacks and pitchers "hold out" for the extra million or two in multimillion-dollar contracts. M.B.A.'s still in their twenties think nothing of asking for and getting salaries in the six figures. To no one's surprise, the circulation of *Money* magazine doubled during the last decade. In America today, we admire the rich and try to forget about the poor.

_____

_____

_____

_____

WORKSHEET 9A   **Beginnings/Endings**

Name _____

REVISION PRACTICE 1

Try to improve several of the following wordy, awkward, or colorless *titles*. Discuss the results with a group or with your class.

The Danger of Sexual Violence to Single, Dating Women
Today's Television Evangelists
Career Choices for Today's Graduates
Afternoon Soap Operas
The Dwindling Supply of Low-Cost Housing
Trends in Health Foods
A Comparison of Home Computers

_____

_____

_____

_____

_____

_____

_____

_____

_____

_____

_____

_____

_____

_____

_____

_____

_____

_____

_____

_____

REVISION PRACTICE 2

Try one of the most familiar ways of ending a paper on a strong note. For a paper on vandalism, graffiti, police brutality or citizen violence, or growing wealth or growing greed, write a conclusion that does one of the following:

- ending with an exceptionally striking or clear-cut example or **case in point**
- turning for confirmation to a **clincher quote** (especially strong clinching quotation) from a witness, expert, or insider
- ending on a **positive note**, giving your readers a realistic suggestion for action or improvement

_____

_____

_____

_____

_____

_____

_____

_____

_____

_____

_____

_____

_____

_____

_____

_____

_____

_____

_____

_____

_____

_____

_____

CAPSULE RULE Use transitional expressions as thought links to guide the reader from point to point.

A **transition** builds a bridge from one point to the next. You might think of it as a ramp that guides your reader from one stretch of road to the next. Transitions show connections—they show your readers how the different parts of your paper fit together. They guide the reader who needs to know:

- Where are we headed?
- What is next?
- What does this prove?
- Does anyone disagree?
- What was the result?

Show logical connections like the following:

EXAMPLE OR ILLUSTRATION:
for example, for instance, to illustrate
MORE OF SAME—additional examples:
similarly, moreover, furthermore
OBJECTION—going on to an opposing point:
however, but, nevertheless
EMPHASIS—highlighting a point:
indeed, in fact, above all
ORDER OF IMPORTANCE (or TIME):
first, second, third; next, finally
LOGICAL CONCLUSION:
therefore, so, consequently, as a result
CONTRAST:
on the contrary, by contrast, on the other hand
CONCESSION—conceding an opposing argument or admitting something:
granted, admittedly, it is true that

PROBLEM SPOTTER

A student writes about the "rugged healthy young males that appear in cigarette ads or beer commercials." He goes on to say that "**Another interesting type** is the retired Hollywood actor who now does insurance commercials aimed at the elderly or at veterans. . . . **Another interesting type** is the handsome middle-aged doctor who recommends cold tablets or pain killers." Is there any connection among the different types?

MISSING LINKS FILLED IN: The stereotypical handsome rugged males dear to American advertising can count on a life-time career.

- **First,** they appear in cigarette ads or beer commercials. . . .
- **Later, in middle age,** they peddle aspirin and cold tablets. . . .
- **Finally, at retirement age,** they peddle insurance to the elderly. . . .

YOUR TURN

See if you can set up a similar three-point or four-point sequence for one of the following: top models, movie actors or actresses, college students, Internet companies, popular singers, or another group that might move through similar stages. Introduce each stage with a transitional expression.

_____

_____

_____

_____

_____

_____

_____

INSTANT REVIEW

Study the *turning points* in the following excerpts of sample student papers.

SAMPLE PAPER 1:   The Aging Student Body

THESIS: **The traditional college campus populated by 18-year-old Joe Colleges and Betty Coeds is a thing of the past.**

Today's college students are on the average older and more experienced than they were in the past. **It is true that** many students still go to college straight from high school. . . .

However, today students often interrupt their schooling to go to work. . . .

A special case is the re-entry woman, who often has dealt with both work and raising a family before finishing college. . . .

As a result, the average age of students is likely to be 28 or 31 rather than 19. . . .

SAMPLE PAPER 2:   The Right to Bear Arms

THESIS: **Many Americans consider the right to bear arms one of their most inalienable rights.**

Americans have traditionally been proud of the right to bear arms. The Second Amendment assures citizens of this right. . . .

However, the language of the amendment must be understood in its historical context. It talks about a "well-regulated militia" or citizen army. . . .

Apart from its constitutional support, the American attachment to guns is firmly rooted in the lore of the West and the frontier. . . .

Today, the basic plot in much of our television and movie entertainment has the bad guys and the police, or terrorists and swat teams, shooting it out. . . .

Not surprisingly, the sound of gunfire is heard just as frequently in our city streets. . . .

Compared with other industrialized countries, our annual rate of homicides involving firearms is appalling. . . .

Nevertheless, gun control legislation always faces fierce political opposition. . . .

In view of our past record, the outlook for a gun-free environment is not good.

Name _____

REVISION PRACTICE
   In each of the following, what is your choice of the missing link? Enter the letter of the right choice on the right.

1   The law restricts searches and seizures. _____ evidence of drug dealing is hard to produce in court.

   a Therefore,   **b** On the other hand,   **c** Similarly,   _____

2   Respect for human life is eroding. _____ drive-by shootings of innocent bystanders are becoming common.

   a Nevertheless,   **b** For example,   **c** But   _____

3   We don't always read the books we buy. _____ some books go directly from bookstore to bookshelf, bypassing the reader's brain.

   a In fact,   **b** Granted,   **c** Nevertheless,   _____

4   Widely publicized studies link heart disease to cholesterol. _____ some researchers question these findings.

   a Therefore,   **b** In fact,   **c** However,   _____

5   Newspapers print much that is trivial. _____ a newspaper in Pennsylvania started to print pet obituaries.

   a However,   **b** As a result,   **c** For instance,   _____

6   The search for new sources of energy has proved disappointing. _____ solar energy is used here and there around the country.

   a For example,   **b** Moreover,   **c** It is true that   _____

7   Alternative energy for a time was a buzzword. _____ we hear little these days about other highly touted advances.

   a Similarly,   **b** However,   **c** In fact,   _____

8   No one seems eager to put up wind-driven generators on wind-swept hilltops. _____ we hear little about tide-driven power stations.

   a On the other hand   **b** However,   **c** Similarly,   _____

9   Costs were often prohibitive. _____ producing oil from shale rock proved very expensive.

   a For instance,   **b** On the other hand,   **c** Therefore,   _____

10   No one anymore sings the praises of nuclear energy. _____ power companies are abandoning billion-dollar nuclear plants.

   a Granted,   **b** Furthermore,   **c** On the contrary,   _____

CAPSULE RULE   Use your paragraphs to make related details add up, and state your key idea in a topic sentence.

A paragraph is a group of sentences that gives you a chance to focus on one part of a subject. Paragraph breaks say to your reader: "Let's clear up this part of it, and then we'll move on."

A good paragraph helps your readers move forward one point at a time. Readers get lost when a paragraph presents many details that do not add up. When writing or revising a paragraph, take time to ask: "What is the point?" The answer to this question will be your **topic sentence.** Usually the topic sentence is the first or second sentence of a paragraph. It lets your readers know early what you are trying to show or what you are trying to prove. They can then look at the examples or reasons you offer in support.

Your basic paragraph-writing skill is to make a point and then offer convincing supporting examples or other material to back up your point:

SAMPLE PARAGRAPH:
   Many Americans today try techniques for counteracting stress. Some try special breathing exercises—long rhythmic deep inhaling and exhaling—when they first get up in the morning. Some study yoga and practice its meditation and relaxation techniques. These coordinate specific body positions and movements with ways of blocking out stressful thoughts. Others listen to subliminal relaxation tapes while driving their cars. Audio tapes with sounds of the forest or of the surf are popular, soothing frazzled nerves after a hard day at the office.

BACKUP EXPLANATION
There is no format that fits every paragraph. Look for variations like the following:

■ Instead of lining up several related examples, the writer may rely on **one extended example** to drive home the key point:

ONE KEY EXAMPLE:
   The aliens in early science fiction movies were usually hostile invaders. They may have seemed benevolent at first, but eventually they turned out to be evil. In one early movie, the aliens offer to carry any earthling who is interested away to a better life on their home planet. Then the people on earth happen to obtain a book by the aliens. When it is translated from the aliens' language, it turns out to be a cookbook giving advice on how to prepare and serve human beings.

■ Not every paragraph has a topic sentence at or near the beginning. Some start with a question that the rest of the paragraph answers. Some leave the main point implied rather than spelled out. Study the following example of a paragraph with the **topic sentence last.**

TOPIC SENTENCE LAST:
   When two gorillas quarrel, they may stare at each other till one of them gives in and shifts his eyes away. Chimps make rough tools from twigs in order to get at food. They greet each other with kisses and cuddles. Although apes do not have voice boxes that would enable them to make speech sounds, they have been taught dozens of signs from the sign language of the deaf, using hand signals to convey their needs and feelings. **The gap that separates apes from humans is not as big as we used to think.**

PROBLEM SPOTTER

What is the point of the following paragraph?

POINT MISSING: If you stop smoking, you may avoid later development of lung cancer or heart disease. If you cut down on drinking, you lower the risk of liver disease. A diet low in fat and calories reduces the risk of heart attacks and diabetes. Watching your cholesterol may reduce the risk of heart attacks and strokes.

POINT ADDED: **How you live now can make a real difference to your future health.** If you stop smoking, you may avoid later development of lung cancer or heart disease. If you cut down on drinking, you lower the risk of liver disease. A diet low in fat and calories reduces the risk of heart attacks and diabetes. Watching your cholesterol may reduce the risk of heart attacks and strokes.

What is the point of the following observations?

POINT MISSING: When nurses put on their nurses' uniforms, they turn into people who efficiently and uncomplainingly respond to requests from patients and physicians. When police officers put on their uniforms, they turn into people who are on the lookout for trouble and violations of the law. When soldiers put on their uniforms, they turn into people who in an emergency would shoot to kill.

POINT ADDED: **When we put on a uniform, we take on a role with definite responsibilities and a code of behavior.** When nurses put on their nurses' uniforms, they turn into people who efficiently and uncomplainingly respond to requests from patients and physicians. When police officers put on their uniforms, they turn into people who are on the lookout for trouble and violations of the law. When soldiers put on their uniforms, they turn into people who in an emergency would shoot to kill.

INSTANT REVIEW

Which of the three sentences that follow each paragraph would be the best topic sentence for the paragraph? Circle the letter of the best choice for topic sentence:

1 _____. Wolves and coyotes used to be considered "varmint" to be trapped and killed, but today we think of ways to help protect these creatures. Many people criticize the killing of animals for their furs. There has been public revulsion against the clubbing of baby seals for their pelts. Dog fanciers have changed their standards to make barbaric practices like ear-cropping obsolete.

    a We have changed our minds about predatory animals of the wild.
    b We are becoming more aware of our kinship with the animals that share the planet with us.
    c Do-gooders are interfering with the traditional rights of hunters.

2 _____. A legendary figure like Buffalo Bill used to be a symbol of the rugged independence of the Western frontier. Today we remember him mostly as one of the people who destroyed the American buffalo. Whereas the tribes of the plains had regarded the buffalo with almost religious reverence, hunters like Buffalo Bill started the wholesale slaughter of the herds and destroyed the livelihood of the Native Americans. He was also notorious as a killer of the natives themselves.

    a Buffalo Bill is one of the best-loved figures of American folklore.
    b The great herds of buffalo that roamed the plains are no more.
    c In recent years, traditional heroes like Buffalo Bill have been taken down from their pedestals.

Name _____

REVISION PRACTICE

A   For each of the following paragraphs, write a more pointed topic sentence to replace the weak opening sentence:

1   *A few years back, newspaper readers read about amazing goings-on.* A quarterback for a football team was signed to a contract worth 17 million dollars. A supporting player on another football team said that he was soon going to be the first million-dollar-a-year member of the defensive secondary. A television evangelist paid himself a million and a half in yearly salary and bonuses. Television announcers reading copy prepared by their staff signed million-dollar contracts.

(So what was amazing about this trend?)

_____

_____

_____

_____

2   *Sharks are amazing.* They can smell blood a quarter of a mile away, and they follow the scent to their prey. They sense motion in the water and will track down someone thrashing about. They are sensitive to bright light and they will head straight for the reflection from the shiny scaly surface of large fish.

(So what is really amazing about sharks?)

_____

_____

_____

_____

3   *Average college students do not take good care of themselves.* They seldom eat a healthful nutritious breakfast. They take in far too much sugar in cookies, candy bars, and soft drinks. Even the yogurt they eat is mostly sugar. They pick themselves up with a quick fix of high-caffeine coffee or Coke. They eat junk foods deficient in vitamins and minerals. They consume large quantities of potato chips rich in cheap fat.

(So what specifically does this paragraph show?)

_____

_____

_____

_____

B For each paragraph, circle the letter of the added example that would be the best choice to strengthen the paragraph.

1   **High-tech medicine has made possible operations undreamed of fifty years ago.** Heart transplants are not yet routine, but they no longer make front-page news. Doctors perform kidney transplants as soon as donors become available. Bypasses repair the damage done by heart attacks that could have proved fatal earlier in this century. _____

   a You never know what medical science will come up with next.
   b Doctors operate on newborn babies for birth defects that in earlier years would have crippled the child for life.
   c Even before the arrival of the Europeans, Mayans in Central America performed surgical operations.

2   **Women today work in many occupations that were once considered sanctuaries for the male of the species.** People have become accustomed to seeing police women and women as members of the armed forces. Female lawyers and judges are everywhere in our courts of law. As the many women now enrolled in medical school graduate, female physicians will become commonplace. _____

   a The choice of a career is one of the most important decisions young people have to make.
   b Many employers are under pressure to provide better job opportunities for America's minorities.
   c Slowly, women are moving into the top management positions that are among the last bastions of white male privilege.

CAPSULE RULE Track the main points and the supporting evidence or examples in what you read.

Writers respond to what they read. They read about events that confirm or challenge their ideas on issues important to them. For instance, they react to what they read about school reform, public transportation, violent video games, or gun control. They take in statistics—about high school dropouts, about legal and illegal immigration, or about the earnings of women or minorities. Many writers file away much of what they read for future use—for support for a pet project or for ammunition in an ongoing argument.

What are the main points in the following reading selection? As a reader, do you agree with the author and want to cheer him on? Or do you want to question him and talk back?

WRITING OPTION

Pretend you have been asked to follow Jimmy Breslin on the podium to address the same audience as a fellow student. Prepare a rough draft of your remarks, for feedback by peers and your instructor.

The following article is excerpted from New York columnist Jimmy Breslin's commencement address to graduates of the City University of New York (CUNY) on June 7, 1999. Breslin is a Pulitzer Prize–winning columnist with *Newsday*. His remarks were circulated informally by friends of the university and were reprinted in part in the July 5, 1999, issue of the *Nation*. Breslin started his talk tongue-in-cheek by addressing the graduates as "frauds"—since many of the attacks on the city university system had called the education and the degrees offered there substandard or fraudulent. The urban university system in New York had long been the center of a debate over "open admission"—giving every student a chance at a college education regardless of whether or not their previous schooling had given them the preparation that is the birthright of every American.

Who Goes to College?

And I come here and discover that you are merely another fraud in the city university system. Of the 150 receiving degrees today, you hold only 191 jobs. That is less than two jobs per student. Oh, there are one or two who have three jobs but they represent a weak attempt to improve the class average. And the scandal is that some of your second jobs are only part time. You don't even have the guts to hold two regular jobs.

What right, then, do you have to take five and six years and more to get a degree? Just because Father didn't leave an estate in proper order is no excuse. Before coming out here, I worked the crowd and I found a couple of women who were receiving—food stamps! They want to feed their grubby little kids or some aging grandmother while they go to a city university. The mayor and the Rand Corporation should be told immediately. I know the mayor is terribly uncomfortable with anybody who isn't white and, therefore, looking out over some of you, can see why he must start frothing when he thinks:

These people are going to make it!
Going to? Good Lord, they already have!
They will wreck my citywide plan for them and their families.
My plan is to teach them how to do nothing!

I can't stand here today and tell you to go forth into the world because you've already done that. In fact, there is virtually nothing that I can say to you when I know of the burdens you have carried for so long and so far and so heroically. I see here today the indescribable beauty of people who make this city the place that tries so mightily to show the world how to try to live. For you bring to us today the greatest, most precious knowledge that you gained here in this university system.

You learned not to quit.
You learned to persevere.
You learned not to whine.
And you learned how simple minded and foolish and harmful it is to condemn anything that you
    have not experienced yourself or through someone else.

You've learned academic courses. On the way in here some person among you handed me the forty items in the CUNY mathematics assessment test. It stressed that, "A student who has been away from mathematics for any length of time is not likely to pass the test." Of course I didn't have time to sit down and do the test. I think that all elected officials in the City of New York should take this test so we can see how smart they are. I also think that they all should write an essay, without cheap press agents doing it for them, so we can see their wonderful grammar.

I never understood what the phrase "thirsting for knowledge" was about. It is a phrase for another world. In this universe here, you know you need to learn in order to survive, to feed children, to hold onto jobs. And you know you must fight your way to every book, every class, every hour of study. You suffer to gain knowledge from a college level. It turns you into rock-hard people who must learn and won't stop until they do.

You have children at home and jobs to pay for their care. And something out there is attracting you, calling to you:

Just keep working.
Working, working, working.
And they close the local libraries of your city in your tired faces.
They don't buy enough books for your schools.

They want anybody in a family off any public assistance and out weeding along the highways. They want you off any assistance to finish school and down in the subways on work gangs that replace people with jobs. If some of those people want to go to school, they are told, "Just pick up broken bottles and be satisfied."

You came this far without advice from some cheap speaker. But it does appear that you have the will and the strength and the flame, and out there they live in fear, and they try to use statistics that lie, and there can be no way that you cannot grind them down and get to where you want to go, to where you rightfully belong. You have so much that we need. You must not be denied.

—Jimmy Breslin

Name _____

How careful a reader are you? Answer the following questions about the commencement speech:

1   Breslin is a speaker who strongly identifies with his **audience.** Unlike the New York politicians he criticizes, Breslin expresses solidarity with students who are not all from affluent middle-class backgrounds. What would you include in a *capsule portrait* of these students?

_____

_____

_____

_____

_____

2   As a central part of his **message**, Breslin congratulates the graduates on gaining knowledge different from what is covered in many standard college courses. According to him, what is the most "precious knowledge" they have gained?

_____

_____

_____

_____

_____

3   Breslin is outspoken in his criticism of the **opposition.** How and why does he attack them? According to Breslin, what is the attitude of conservative politicians toward the students he describes?

_____

_____

_____

_____

_____

4 Critics like Breslin claim that **tests** and testing organizations hold back or flunk out minorities or students in need of help instead of advancing their cause. (Why or how?) Where and how does Breslin attack the emphasis on tests in this speech?

_____

_____

_____

_____

_____

_____

5 There has been much media discussion of what is wrong with American education. Toward the end, Breslin strongly attacks society's neglect of the schools. What are key points in his indictment?

_____

_____

_____

_____

_____

_____

FOLLOWING UP: EDITORIAL WRITER FOR A DAY

In a companion article published in the same issue of the *Nation,* Patrick S. Lane, a faculty member at the Bernard M. Baruch College of the City University of New York, made the following claims. If you had been invited by a New York newspaper to write a **guest editorial** as student representative, what would you say?

- Only one of the fifty states spends less on its colleges and universities than it did ten years ago—New York.
- With stable levels of enrollment from 1976 to 1996, the number of full-time faculty was cut in half and replaced with part-time "adjunct" faculty.
- The Republican governor and the Republican mayor turned down all three finalists for the job of heading the CUNY system, although they were chosen by the search committee of the CUNY Board of Trustees.
- In the debate over the future of CUNY, the needs of 150,000 nondegree, continuing-education students had been largely ignored.

CAPSULE RULE **Draw on your own firsthand experience and observation.**

Much of the world we live in we know only at second hand. We rely on the spin news-casters give to the news. We trust what textbooks tell us, or we believe a teacher's account of events in history. However, we often do our strongest writing when we go beyond second-hand ideas to what we have seen with our own eyes. We then write as witnesses, trying to understand and share with others what mattered in our own lives.

Read and study the following student paper. Do you agree that the writer writes honestly about something that really happened—something that mattered? Do you think that others may find it worth thinking about and perhaps learn something from it?

- What for you stands out most in this paper?
- What details or incidents are you most likely to remember?
- Do you think this is a familiar story—or is it a story about someone with a special or unusual problem?
- Does the paper remind you of anything in your own experience?
- What do you think a reader should learn from this student's story?

Write a *letter to the student author*, sharing your reactions to what the student wrote.

One Person's Influence

I used to live with a man whose stern outer expressions always masqueraded his innermost feelings. Whether happy, sad, or mad, he always seemed to have the same grim look on his face. Even the inclination in his deep voice never wavered. He always projected his statements in the same curt manner. This man's intimidating "hello" used to cause my older cousin to hang up the telephone in fright.

This man is my stepfather, and I still remember how his harsh dark brown eyes used to strike at me like a fierce arrow, piercing me down, the aim of his target. I would cringe at his stare, feeling my already tiny six-year-old body diminish under the kitchen table in an attempt to escape. With no words, he communicated his message through a glare. It commanded, "You're not getting up from this table until you eat everything on your plate." As I forced the bland vegetables down my palate, fighting the horrible urge to gag and vomit these greens and yellows all over my plate, I would stare at him. I would scan his wrinkled forehead and his salt-and-peppered mustache but always manage to dodge his eyes.

My mother had a very different way of parenting, the more modernized theory of "Try it and if you don't like, it you don't have to eat it." Yet of course, there were times when my mother wasn't home and I was forced to fend for myself. This may seem trivial or simplistic, but to a first-grader, vegetables and a seemingly scary old man are serious issues. Not to mention, this slight parenting technicality caused much tension and debate between the two adults.

Growing up, I was very close to my mother, but with my stepfather it was quite a different story. Even the way I addressed him signifies our relationship, or lack thereof. I didn't call him "Dad" as if he were a father figure to me. I didn't even refer to him as an informal Bob, as if he were a friend. Rather, I called him a formal, distant name: Robert. We lived in a relatively small house, three bedrooms in all. Yet the gap between us stretched on for endless miles. Our words spoken to each other were meaningless—just sounds in the empty air. We talked only when necessary, chit chat at dinner and a hello or goodbye here and there. I never sat on his lap while he told me a story. We never hugged and never kissed. I never questioned this mutual behavior. For the longest time, I just figured this was the norm. This is how it's supposed to be when you have a stepdad.

Perhaps what was most bewildering was the fact that my stepdad was not incapable of a caring affectionate relationship. On the contrary, he did express these sorts of feelings, not to me however, but to our dogs. Funny as it may seem, it's very true. Robert really felt a deep and excessive love for our two beautiful dogs. He loved playing with the dogs, hugging them and rolling on the ground with them. He bought them fancy collars, extravagant leashes, and expensive toys, which ended up being eaten in a week's time. He took off from work to bring them to the doctor's and ensured their health by preparing them well-rounded meals. He cooked chicken and rice and mixed the recipe with name brand dog food, vegetable oil for shiny coats, vitamins E and C to prevent sickness, and brewer's yeast to fight off fleas.

At the age of ten or eleven, I felt jealous. Now, I just have questions. How can a man love a canine more than a child? How can he wake up at three in the morning, without any complaints or even a grumble, to open the back door for a dog, yet anger so easily when fifteen minutes after ten, my phone rang and woke him up?

My stepdad's influence on my life hasn't been all bad. I'm now a young adult, and I have adjusted to the barrier between us. I don't even mind getting into confrontations with my stepfather. I like voicing my opinion, making it loud and clear that it's different than his, and sometimes we even agree. He never succeeded in making me like all my vegetables, but I can now look him in the eye. I did learn from him that not everyone is going to understand me.

I must admit that a few times in the years that I've known him, my stepfather has surprised me. He brought me to my first Golden Gate Warriors' game, just the two of us. On a rainy day at Pier 39, he let me wear his hooded jacket. I hold on tight to these isolated incidents. I still have the tickets to the game and a borrowed jacket.

Name _____

Would you find it hard or easy to write a paper like the following about people important to your life? (What kind of response would you prepare for the student author?) Prepare a **journal entry** that could be the first step toward a similar paper.

My Parents' Career

When a teacher asks a student what his or her parent's occupation is, you would think that it would be easy to answer. Usually the answers ranged from lawyer to a nurse but my answer was always different, confusing, and unexplainable. My parents do not have an occupation that everyone understands. For many years of my life, I couldn't explain it to myself. It was even hard for my parents to explain to others that they were and are Catholic missionaries who move around going to church and church forming Christian communities (within the Catholic Church) and evangelizing the Word of God.

It took me a long time to accept the job that my parents took up almost twelve years ago. Growing up as a traveling child had its hardships. I would walk into a different class full with staring children, who unlike me had already settled down for the year, and a teacher that introduced me as the newcomer of the class, every three or four months. I had to learn to adapt to many soft, hard, stiff, or comfortable different beds and suffer the bruises of bumping into walls when I got up in the middle of the night to go to the bathroom. When I finally had gotten used to the new house and the new school with new friends, it was time to leave. I never liked having to leave the friends I made along the way nor the memories I had of all the places I had lived in. But most of all I hated starting all over. It was as if I had to be born again every three months.

One of the hardest years for me when we were moving around was my eighth-grade year, the year of my graduation from grammar school. I had always planned to finish in the school which I had started in, which was in Los Angeles, but deep down I knew that that would not happen. Four months before graduation it was time to move again but this time I wasn't going to the usual school I went to when I moved to San Francisco; I was going to move into a whole new different school. The night before I started I cried myself to sleep trying desperately to find a scapegoat for all that had happened so far in my life. The next morning, as it had become a tradition for my family, I started a new school with new children staring at me as my teacher introduced me as the newcomer.

That year it was really hard for me to fit with the crowd and I ended up getting into many fights, but all of it was based on the fact that all the students in my class had been together for years and as I made friends with one person, I destroyed a relationship between another. During my eighth-grade year and most of my other schooling years traveling made it hard for me to create a relationship with another person that I could call a true friend. Although I never had this problem, I often tried to open up to people who I thought would understand who I really was and what my family was all about, but no matter how I tried to understand no one really understood.

Many times I would sit next to my window on a rainy day and desperately seek a solution to what had become a problem. I would often blame God for everything that happened to me. I blamed Him for everything that I did not have as a child and for everything that I did not have at that moment. I knew that if my father had kept his job as an electrician he would be earning at least thirty dollars an hour and I would have had everything that I desired and that I never got as a child for lack of money.

Out of the twelve years my parents have been missionaries, it took me eight years to understand and appreciate the work they have done. I learned to comprehend what my parents' job really entailed through evangelizing, moving around, and changing people's lives. During my high school career I began to find an answer to that question that I have always asked myself. Everything that has happened to my family has created the person I am today. I have learned to adapt quickly to new atmospheres, I have become determined to be different from everyone else, and I have become a strong person with a strong sense of morals. I realized that my family had been chosen to do this job for a unique purpose, one that many might not understand. Understanding the mission that my parents had helped me understand that my life could not have been better. There are not many young adults that can say that they have traveled the world.

UNIT 13   ■   *Writing from Experience*

CAPSULE RULE Use major writing/thinking strategies to organize your papers.

What kind of thinking goes into organizing a paper? Organizing strategies like the following will help you lay out material so that it will be instructive or informative. Use them alone or in combination.

- **PROCESS** How does it work? Trace a process (baking bread; coping with divorce) through several major stages. Show your readers what it takes or what it took to make a process work.
- **COMPARISON/CONTRAST** How are two things alike? How are they different? Chart similarities and differences. For instance you might look at electioneering then and now. In the past, an election centered on personal appearances, rallies, and volunteer workers. Today, more and more the key roles are played by canned TV spots, focus groups, and paid campaign workers.
- **CLASSIFICATION** What goes with what? Set up major categories to help readers find their way. For instance look at local politics in urban, suburban, and rural America. (Is big-city politics different from suburban politics and again from upstate or back country politics?) Or look at motivation in team sports, single-competitor sports, and noncompetitive sports.

BACKUP EXPLANATION

Organizing a paper does not require a different special kind of thinking. We do not put on a special thinking hat when we sit down at the computer to write a paper. A historian charting major stages in the settling of the West and a developer explaining the major stages in creating a new apartment complex both do **process analysis:** They cut up a continuous process into major phases so we can concentrate on one major stage at a time.

Comparison and classification both mirror the way our minds process information. **Classification** papers may use familiar, well-established categories—like describing upper class sports, middle class sports , and working class sports, for instance. But often they require us to redraw boundaries or chart new territory—for instance *subdividing* the working class into full-time workers, part-time workers, and the "unemployable" chronically unemployed.

PROBLEM SPOTTER

A student writer talks about some of the changes in the workplace from her parents' generation to hers, but they do not add up. They do not fall into a pattern. What is the solution? The student writer sorts out the material, setting up major categories and clearly showing the contrast between then and now. The result is a **point-by-point** comparison:

The Changing Workplace

	(THEN)	(NOW)
KIND OF WORK:	heavy manual labor	dealing with people
WORKING ENVIRONMENT:	dirty unsafe conditions	computer-assisted work
CHIEF COMPLAINT:	repetitive tasks	electronic monitoring

53

Or the writer may choose to describe past and present separately but take up the same points in **parallel order.** For each period, we then get the "whole picture"—but we may have to make more of an effort to see the connections:

The Changing Workplace

(THEN)

KIND OF WORK:	heavy manual labor
WORKING ENVIRONMENT:	dirty unsafe conditions
CHIEF COMPLAINT:	repetitive tasks

(NOW)

KIND OF WORK:	dealing with people
WORKING ENVIRONMENT:	computer-assisted work
CHIEF COMPLAINT:	electronic monitoring

INSTANT REVIEW

Study the following **working outlines,** and be prepared to discuss them with other students. How clear is each outline? What is the major organizing strategy for each? What details or examples does it make you expect?

OUTLINE 1:   Back to the Country

I   Drawbacks of city life

  A   Anonymity (lonely in a crowd)
  B   Paranoia (fear of violence, suspicion of strangers)
  C   Congestion (traffic jams, no parking)
  D   Pollution

II   Advantages of country life

  A   Neighborliness (mutual assistance)
  B   Peace of mind
  C   Open spaces
  D   Fresh air

OUTLINE 2:   Fresh from the Lab to You

Ways we tamper with natural crops and fruit:

- genetic engineering for ease of handling
  (preferred shapes for packing or transport)
- enzymes for convenience of harvesting
  (with fruit all ripening at the same time)
- chemical additives for better appearance
  (coloring, etc.)
- added artificial flavors

OUTLINE 3:   Women in the Media: Emerging from the Stereotype

- the airhead housewife (*I Love Lucy*)
- the sexy detective (*Charlie's Angels*)
- the tough avenger (Sigourney Weaver in *Alien*)

Name _____

WRITING PRACTICE

1   The following sample outline sets up *three major categories* of law-breaking. For each category, can you fill in briefly some examples from your observation, viewing, or reading? (You may change the categories if you think they need to be adjusted.) Prepare to share your material for feedback from your instructor or peers.

The Tip of the Crime Wave

THESIS: Street crime is part of a larger pattern; it illustrates a mindset that also makes other kinds of crime possible.

FIRST CATEGORY: Street crime—muggings, stabbings, car thefts

_____

_____

_____

_____

_____

SECOND CATEGORY: White-collar crime—embezzlement, investment scams, insider trading, corruption

_____

_____

_____

_____

_____

THIRD CATEGORY: Personal dishonesty—petty theft, "ripping off" employers, cheating on taxes

_____

_____

_____

_____

_____

2 The following is an incomplete trial outline for a *parallel-order comparison/contrast* of the single life and the married life. How would you complete the outline? If necessary, how would you change the original entries? Make sure the second part of the outline takes up the same or similar issues in parallel order. Change or rearrange entries as you wish.

Then prepare notes or a rough first draft for a paper following this or a similar blueprint.

Till Divorce Do Us Part

I The single lifestyle

  A Control over your own money

  B Budgeting your own time

  C Irregular eating habits

  D _____

II The married lifestyle

  A Pooling financial resources

  B _____

  C _____

  D _____

_____

_____

_____

_____

_____

_____

_____

_____

_____

_____

_____

_____

_____

_____

_____

CAPSULE RULE Expand your range of words used in discussing issues and ideas.

In the following newspaper article, some words are **technical words** or specialist's words. The specialist has to explain them to ordinary readers. For instance, this article explains names for diseases or disabilities and for new technological marvels that help people cope with them. However, many other words are words that help the **general reader** join in the discussion of issues and ideas. Pay special attention to the boldfaced terms in the following article. Which of these are familiar? Which are new to you? Which can you make out from the **context**—the way they are used in the sentence or larger paragraph?

The author of the following article was the editor of a weekly newsmagazine in Philadelphia until her disability made it more and more difficult for her to communicate.

Harnessing Brain Waves

Medford, New Jersey

When the average person turns on the computer, the **ubiquitous** Windows screen appears. The little **icons** flash as programs load and within seconds, you're ready to go. For people like me who are severely disabled due to accidents, diseases, or birth defects, the process that allows us to use a computer is just beginning. After the regular programs load, my screen turns blue, the **logo** "Words +, E Z Keys for Windows" appears and, in bold black letters, UNLOCKING THE PERSON. Technology is giving us back a voice.

The system I use was developed by California-based Words + for **astrophysicist** Stephen Hawking who, like me, has amyotrophic lateral sclerosis (ALS), also known as Lou Gehrig Disease. The **progressive** disease eventually causes loss of all skeletal muscle function, which means we can't speak or operate a keyboard. We need what are called augmentative communications devices. These have been developed in various forms over the last **decade**, mainly using computers. One of the best-known types is called Dragon Dictate. All the operator needs is a voice. **Verbal** commands are translated into keyboard commands or text. The text can also be read back by the computer.

Actor Christopher Reeve was shown using this type of no-hands system in the recent remake of the movie "Rear Window." It is a popular program for the blind and, more and more, it's being used by people who just don't want to use a keyboard, for whatever reason. There are even systems that require only eye movement to operate. With names like VisionKey and Eye-gaze, their main drawback, other than expense, is the **cumbersomeness** of the equipment, which must be carefully **calibrated**. It's not something you take with you, like a PC. As wonderful as all these devices are, there has remained a bar to communicating that defied technology until recently: how to communicate when "locked in."

When ALS progresses to its final stage, even the eyes don't move. Victims of severe stroke may have the same problem. The brain functions, but there is no way to contact the world outside. Researchers in four places—Atlanta and Albany in this country, and in Germany and Japan—have been reporting remarkable success with brain wave communications—brain to computer. The basic **principle**, straight out of Star Trek, is that brain wave activity can be **harnessed** and trained to move a **cursor** or arrow on a computer screen to indicate words. Drs. Roy Bakay and Philip Kennedy at Emory University in Atlanta have developed the most **complex** method. They implant a small device in the brain, along with neurotrophic chemicals that stimulate nerves to grow and connect with the device. A coil is then placed on the top of the head and the subject begins training to move the cursor on a computer screen. Dr. Jonathan Wolpaw, of the Wadsworth Center at the State University of New York in Albany, uses a **non-invasive** cap with 64 electronic **sensors** that fits like a bathing cap.

With training, the subject uses mental energy to access the brain's "mu rhythm." Wolpaw claims upward of 90 percent accuracy spelling words and answering yes/no questions. In Germany, Dr. Niels Birbaumer of the University of Tuebingen heads a group that claims 95 percent accuracy harnessing another kind of brain wave called "slow cortical potentials." Perhaps the most unusual research is being done by an electronics engineer in Japan, Hidenori Ohnishi. His portable device is called MCTOS, for Mind Controlled Tool Operating System. As word of his success spread among the ALS community, dozens of e-mails were sent to Japan begging for his help. Earlier this year, at his own expense, he visited two of his U.S. **correspondents**, in Grand Rapids, Michigan, and in Bailey, Colorado. Not only was his device reported as successful with the two ALS patients, but also with a five-year-old girl with the **genetic** disease, metachromatic leukocyte. Within minutes, his **subjects** could turn a chime on and off by "changing conscious brainwave activity to an excited state," according to observer Carl Brahe, of Bailey. He reported 100 percent success with three ALS patients, two genetically **impaired** children and three teenagers paralyzed from car accidents.

—Dale O. Reilley

YOUR TURN

For each item in the worksheet that follows, go back to the article to find the word that fits the context. Write it in the space provided. If the word is new or confusing for you, discuss the way it is used with your classmates.

Name _____

Go back to the article to find the missing word, and fill it in the space provided.

1 **EXAMPLE:** Features of computers seen everywhere are _____**ubiquitous**_____.

2 Small symbols for limited computer functions are _____.

3 A symbol with a larger meaning is called a _____.

4 A physicist studying star systems is an _____.

5 A disease that keeps getting worse is a _____ disease.

6 A period of ten years is called a _____.

7 Commands given by voice are _____ commands.

8 Devices that are very awkward to handle are _____.

9 Equipment designed to exact measurements is _____.

10 Each new system has its own key idea or basic _____.

11 Forces that are controlled and put to work are _____.

12 The arrow that shows where you are on the screen is the _____.

13 When complicated features work together, the system is _____.

14 Procedures that enter or invade the subject's body are _____.

15 Sophisticated devices that pick up signals are _____.

16 A device that you can carry with you is _____.

17 People who send mail back and forth are _____.

18 A disease that is inherited is a _____ disease.

19 The patients being studied are called _____.

20 Patients damaged by birth defects or accidents are _____.

INSTANT REVIEW

Circle the letter for the best choice.

		a	b	c
1	portable	a entranceway	b can be carried	c tolerable
2	principle	a main idea	b administrator	c aristocrat
3	genetic	a manipulated	b artificial	c inherited
4	complex	a traditional	b oversimple	c not simple
5	icon	a symbol	b signature	c deceit
6	progressive	a continuing	b in spurts	c looking back
7	decade	a half century	b ten years	c every second year
8	impaired	a badly hurt	b improved	c set up in twos
9	calibrated	a hand-made	b prohibited	c measured exactly
10	verbal	a talkative	b word of mouth	c hearsay

CAPSULE RULE Edit for confusing or inappropriate words.

A   EDITING FOR INACCURATE WORDS

Study the difference between words often confused. If you have trouble with pairs like these, go over them several times.

attribute	We **attribute** a person's success to hard work. (we pay tribute or give credit)
contribute	We **contribute** to charitable organizations. (we make a contribution)
imply	A speaker can **imply** something instead of saying it outright.
infer	The listener can **infer** things not explicitly stated. (we infer what's implied)
let	Many parents **let** their children do as they please.
leave	Few parents **leave** their children altogether. (use **let** to mean allow)
respectfully	The mourners **respectfully** made way for the widow. (they showed respect)
respectively	The widow and her son inherited ten thousand dollars and an apartment house, **respectively.** (the will stipulated something *different* for each person)
teach	Teachers **teach** their students.
learn	Students **learn** something from their teachers. (teachers do not *learn* their students something)
predominate	Anglo students **predominated** on campus. (to *predominate* is something people do)
predominant	Asians were the **predominant** minority. (to be *predominant* is something people are)

INSTANT REVIEW

Look at the italicized words in the following sentences. In which of the sentences is a confusing word used right? Put a check mark next to the sentence.

1   Listening to her, the reporters *inferred* she would run for senator.   _____

2   Money from the new fund would go to the states and cities, *respectively*.   _____

3   Schools should *leave* student editors set their own policies.   _____

4   Although still hedging, the mayor *inferred* that he would run for reelection.   _____

5   Our teachers did not try to *learn* us something new every day.   _____

6   The article *attributed* the quotation to an unnamed source.   _____

7   Latino voters were *predominant* in the district.   _____

8   Students used to treat teachers more *respectively*.   _____

9   Simon seldom *contributed* to class discussion.   _____

10   Farming has been the *predominate* occupation.   _____

EDITING PRACTICE

Look at the italicized part in each of the following sentences. Write down a word or an expression that would give the intended meaning more accurately.

EXAMPLE: If the new city hall is to serve the whole community, it should be *centralized* in the city.

_____**centrally located**_____

1 Often a simple word like "car" can replace a phrase like "motor vehicle," and the same meaning is *portrayed.*

_____

2 He felt that a hands-off policy was the best one for the government *to play.*

_____

3 In some school districts, teachers are forced to *restrain* from voicing their opinions.

_____

4 The freshman student is *affronted* by such problems as selecting a major field of study and choosing among different social activities.

_____

5 The editorial *inferred* that athletes were accepting compensation for work they had never done.

_____

6 *In compliance to* my roommates, I made the call.

_____

7 Lois *dislocated* the document and was unable to find it in spite of a thorough search.

_____

8 Let us hope that in the end common sense will *pervade.*

_____

9 The police, alerted by a neighbor, were able to *comprehend* two of the intruders.

_____

10 Competence alone should be the *judge* whether a teacher should be allowed to teach.

_____

B   EDITING FOR INFORMAL LANGUAGE

The right language for discussion of issues and ideas is serious without being stiff or pretentious. Many expressions are all right for everyday talk but are too **informal** for most college writing. Can you match the informal words in the following sampling with the more serious choice that would be right for most college writing?

INFORMAL: boss, buddy, deal, flop, folks, kid, tyke
MORE FORMAL: **employer, friend, agreement, failure, family, child, small child**
INFORMAL: goof, well-heeled, cop, dope, guts, guy, old man, sucker
MORE FORMAL: **make a mistake, wealthy, police officer, narcotics, courage, male,**
                 husband or lover, dupe

When language becomes *very* informal, it shades over into **slang**. Can you match the slangy words in the following sampling with the more serious choice that would be right for most college writing?

VERY INFORMAL: faze, gyp, flunk, snoop, snooze, enthused, snooty
MORE FORMAL: **disconcert, cheat, fail, pry, nap, enthusiastic, snobbish**

INSTANT REVIEW

Put a check mark next to sentences that are *not* too informal for serious discussion.

1   The kidnapper had threatened to blow away his hostages.   _____

2   Reporters squawked about a conflict of interest.   _____

3   Divorced parents often try to blame each other for the hurt done to their children.   _____

4   The sportswriters said the quarterback was all washed up.   _____

5   In the new stadium, taxpayers paid for luxury boxes for the rich.   _____

6   She knew her supervisor would blow his top if she took the day off.   _____

7   Voter registration is the key to successful electoral politics.   _____

8   Few young Americans vote.   _____

9   The manager was picky about dress and appearance.   _____

10 I told her to stop bugging me about the rent.   _____

EDITING PRACTICE

Each of the following sentences contains an expression that is too informal for serious writing. Write a better choice in the space provided.

1   A person's ideas change in many ways when he begins to associate with the rest of the college *gang.*

    _____

2   Charles was an extremely successful lawyer, though he was somewhat of *a crackpot* in his private life.

    _____

3   Getting a passport at the last minute turned into *a big hassle.*

    _____

4 Because of rain, the parade was a *flop.*

_____

5 After dinner, the mayor introduced one of her *cronies* as the chief speaker of the evening.

_____

6 The new manager was the most *stuck-up* person I had ever met.

_____

7 The new superintendent was a *wimp* who never talked back to the school board.

_____

8 At the assembly, the student body president acted very *enthused* over the new program.

_____

9 When I called the boy's parents, I did not have the *guts* to tell them what had happened.

_____

10 The objective part of the exam was easy, but the essay part *threw me.*

_____

11 The governor *wangled* a deal that allowed the state to retain nominal title to the land.

_____

12 The government talked about the energy crisis for years but never *got its act together.*

_____

INSTANT REWRITE

Rewrite the following passage to make it *less informal* and more appropriate for serious writing:

The founder of this state-wide poll is a throwback to another era. In a laid-back state where people get off on beach parties, he keeps dishing out his poll results and off-the-wall analyses. For many years, he has been a top watchdog, and he has survived disastrous scrapes. His phone rings off the hook at election time when columnists want the scuttlebutt on current candidates. He has had his share of flops and brickbats but also kudos from clients and rivals alike.

_____

_____

_____

_____

_____

CAPSULE RULE   Become sensitive to language that is offensive or demeaning to others.

There is no government agency in charge of enforcing the use of "politically correct" language. However, educated Americans have over the years become increasingly sensitive to language that is offensive or demeaning to others. Few publications anymore will tolerate language that seems to perpetuate ignorant prejudices about Americans identified by ethnicity, gender, sexual orientation, physical condition, or medical history. Many of a new generation of Americans resist routine labeling by group (as if group identity were what most mattered about them) altogether. Others assert their roots in the rich diverse heritage of the American people while insisting on the use of terms that do not carry a heavy freight of racist or sexist bigotry.

A   Study pointers about how to refer to **group identity**—when it is clearly relevant or appropriate to do so. (Remember that many Americans would simply check "Mixed" if census takers and makers of questionnaires provided such a box for them.)

- Widely respected African American writers or artists, as well as leaders in the black community, use **black**, **African American**, or **people of color** (maybe also still **Afro-American**). One of the most prestigious organizations still calls itself by its historical name—NAACP (the National Association for the Advancement of Colored People).

- Mexican Americans (no hyphen) or Puerto Ricans may identify themselves as **Hispanics**—Americans of Spanish-speaking ancestry. (This is the term often used by government agencies and by Anglo politicians who are discovering the voting power of an often bilingual population.) A new generation, remembering the mass destruction of the Spanish conquest of the Americas, prefers **Latino** (male) and **Latina** (female)—named after the Latin of the Roman empire that was the mother language of Spanish and Portuguese as well as Italian and French. In California, **Chicano/Chicana** (short for **Mexicano/Mexicana**) are often used by Californians with strong ties to Mexico.

- Columbus thought he had landed in India when he called the inhabitants of the Caribbean *indios*—Indians. The preferred term today is **Native American**, although many prefer the ancient honorific tribal names for the separate groups—**Lakota, Kiowa, Cheyenne.**

- *Oriental* came to carry a heavy freight of media images of the *sinister Oriental* or *inscrutable Oriental*. The preferred term today is **Asian**. Remember, however, that *Asian* is an umbrella term covering a tremendous range of different ethnicities and cultures—including Filipino, Vietnamese, Chinese, Korean, Japanese, Thai, Pakistani, and others.

- Avoid any and all terms that seem to assign general physical characteristics or alleged predictable behavior patterns to Mexicans, Jews, Irish, or Italians. (If you want to tell jokes, tell them about your own group or ethnicity.)

B Women in particular have in recent years become extremely aware of the assumptions, prejudices, and putdowns built into language about their gender. Avoid language that perpetuates sexist stereotypes. Do not make it sound as if everything really important in your world relates to males.

1 Watch for "man" words—words that use *man* in some way when actually the reference should be **gender-neutral**. It should apply equally to both sexes. In unisex situations, avoid words with *man* in them or with other masculine markers.

MAN-CENTERED:	mankind, the history of man, the best man for the job, man-made, the common man
GENDER-NEUTRAL:	**humanity, the history of human beings, the best person for the job, manufactured, the average person** (or **ordinary people**)

Avoid *occupational labels* that seem to steer men into some professions and shunt women into others. Use a **member of Congress** instead of a *Congressman*.

MAN-CENTERED:	policeman, businessman, fireman, mailman, chairman
GENDER-NEUTRAL:	**police officer, business executive, firefighter, mail carrier, chairperson** (or simply **chair**)

2 Watch for words ending in *-ess*. Do without truly belittling words like *poetess*. But watch out also for *stewardess* or even *waitress*. (Many restaurants now call the people—male or female—who serve you your meals **servers**.) Use **flight attendant** instead of *stewardess*.

3 Many occupational labels in English are already unisex or common-gender nouns: **doctor, manager, secretary, professor,** and **senator**. However, English has no **generic singular pronoun**—no common-gender singular pronoun like *he/she*. As a result, sexist prejudices may resurface when a writer routinely uses *he* or *him* when referring to judges, doctors, and executives but *she* or *her* when referring to secretaries and nurses. Try the following options to correct the stereotyping or the exclusion of women:

- Use the **double pronoun** *he or she* (or *his or her*), unless several of these in a row make a passage awkward:

  SEXIST: A doctor should listen more to *his* nurse, because *she* is closer to *his* patients.

  DOUBLE PRONOUN: A doctor should listen more to **his or her** nurse, who is closer to the patients.

- Change everything to the **plural** (no indication of gender):

  PLURAL: Doctors should listen more to **their** nurses, who are closer to the patients.

- Do *without* the pronoun altogether (no indication of gender):

  NO PRONOUN: Doctors should listen more to nurses, who are closer to the patients.

Name _____

PROBLEM SPOTTER

What was the problem in each of the following sentences? How was it resolved?

NO: A police chief has to teach his men to be more sensitive to community needs.
YES: **A police chief has to teach his or her officers to be more sensitive to community needs.**

NO: When an accused teacher goes to her principal, he may not have the courage to support her.
YES: **When accused teachers go to the principal, he or she may not have the courage to support them.**

NO: A Congressman who wants to be chairman of a committee has to humor the leadership.
YES: **A member of Congress who wants to chair a committee has to humor the leadership.**

NO: In the history of man's rise from barbarism, the focus has often been on kings and generals rather than on the common man.
YES: **In the history of humanity's rise from barbarism, the focus has often been on kings and generals rather than on the common people.**

NO: Every passenger has to have his ticket validated.
YES: **Every passenger has to have his or her ticket validated.**

INSTANT REVIEW

Check for sexist language. Put a check mark after sentences that are satisfactory.

1 The average college student is worried about his grades.   _____

2 A sports writer needs to do more to check his or her sources.   _____

3 An experienced manager shows his appreciation for the girls in the office.   _____

4 The new CEO should be a person of some stature.   _____

5 A few Congressmen from rural districts can shift the balance in the legislature. _____

6 Police officers and firefighters risk their lives for the community.   _____

7 A pilot needs to have good rapport with his stewardesses.   _____

8 An outstanding consultant can make his or her client look brilliant.   _____

9 A father should realize that sometimes the teacher knows more about troubled children than he does.   _____

10 Even a computer specialist knows that his knowledge may be outdated in a few years.   _____

INSTANT REWRITE

Rewrite the following sentences to edit for sexist language.

1 Recent discoveries of remains of early man and of man-made objects tell us more about the history of mankind.

_____

_____

2 The taxpayer expects decent services but votes against better pay for policemen, social workers, and firemen.

_____

_____

3 A teacher who calls for disciplinary action against one of her students often sees him cleared by a principal worried about his job.

_____

_____

4 The chairman has to be the best man for the job, able to talk as an equal with men of substance in the community.

_____

_____

5 A stewardess or secretary is no longer hired just for her looks.

_____

_____

6 Even if he sends his children to a private school, a politician has to appeal to the man in the street.

_____

_____

7 Even when a nurse knows the doctor is wrong, she takes a risk if she goes against his orders.

_____

_____

8 A judge may reveal his opinions and biases in an article in a law journal.

_____

_____

CAPSULE RULE **Do not split off a sentence part that does not have its own subject and verb.**

A complete sentence has a subject and a verb: **Astronauts** (subject) **walked** (verb) on the moon. **Thousands** (subject) **watch** (verb) rocket launchings. **The *Challenger*** (subject) **was** (verb) an ill-fated spacecraft. Look at what is missing in each of the following sentence fragments:

FRAGMENT: The Russians first launched a space satellite. *The Sputnik.*
(no **verb**—what did *the Sputnik do*?)

FRAGMENT: Cosmonauts spent months in space. *Orbiting the earth.*
(no **subject**—*what* was orbiting the earth?)

FRAGMENT: They were married in a nudist camp. *In their natural state.*
(no **subject or verb**—who did what?)

Link such afterthoughts to the sentences that explain who does what or what is what. Do not keep them separate after a period.

COMPLETE: The Russians first launched **a space satellite, the *Sputnik*.**
COMPLETE: Cosmonauts spent months **in space orbiting the earth.**
COMPLETE: They were married **in a nudist camp in their natural state.**

BACKUP EXPLANATION

Look out for common types of fragments:

1 **Prepositional phrases** are added explanations starting with prepositions—linking words like *in, at, by, with, without, to, from, for, about, around, over, under,* and *through.* Tie the added explanation into the main sentence *without any punctuation:*

FRAGMENT: The leaky boat was to take them across the sea. *To freedom.*
COMPLETE: The leaky boat was to take them **across the sea to freedom.**

2 **Appositives** are added labels: our friend, **the doctor;** Ralph Nader, **the consumer advocate;** Sandra O'Connor, **the Supreme Court Justice.** Tie these added labels into the main sentence *with a comma:*

COMPLETE: The Soviets build **the first space station, the *Mir*.**

3 **Verbals** are parts of verbs: **orbiting** is part of *was orbiting;* **broken** is part of *was broken.* Tie these in *without a comma* if they specify which, what, or when:

WHICH ONE? They discovered **a moon orbiting Jupiter.**

Tie verbals into the sentence with a comma if they merely tell us more about something already nailed down:

ADDED DATA: They aimed for **Phobos, orbiting Jupiter.**
ADDED DATA: She had voted for **Clinton, first elected in 1992.**

PROBLEM SPOTTER

Can you explain what the problem was in the original sentence? Can you explain how it was solved?

NO: The Democrats won the election. *By a few thousand votes.*
YES: The Democrats won the election by a few thousand votes.
NO: Moviegoers liked Charles Bronson. *The rugged type.*
YES: Moviegoers liked Charles Bronson, the rugged type.
NO: We were tired of watching Rambo. *Blowing people's brains out.*
YES: We were tired of watching Rambo blowing people's brains out.
NO: They had spent the night on the mountain. *Trapped in a tent.*
YES: They had spent the night on the mountain, trapped in a tent.
NO: The Feds raised interest rates. *To dampen inflation.*
YES: The Feds raised interest rates to dampen inflation.

INSTANT REVIEW

Some headlines are complete sentences. Some are abbreviated, lacking a subject or a verb or both. Put a check mark after each headline that is a complete sentence.

1 The President Vetoes Tax Cut   _____
2 Pollution Hurts Wildlife   _____
3 Garish New Casinos in Vegas   _____
4 Teachers' Salaries Lagging Behind   _____
5 Consumer Groups Challenge Tobacco Companies   _____
6 New Tensions in Desert Country's Divided Capital   _____
7 The County's Treasurer Had Embezzled Millions   _____
8 Investors Fear Market Crash   _____
9 Affordable Child Care Is Hard to Find   _____
10 Startling Prehistoric Cave Paintings Found in the Desert   _____

FINER POINTS

1 Sometimes a **colon** or **dash** is the best way to link an explanation, list, or comment to the main sentence:

FRAGMENT: She had a choice of two jobs. *Design or marketing.*
COLON: She had a choice of **two jobs: design or marketing.**
FRAGMENT: He was trained as a typesetter. *A doomed occupation.*
DASH: He was trained as **a typesetter—a doomed occupation.**

2 Use a comma to hook up fragments caused by **such as, especially,** or **for example.** Put no second comma after **such as** or **especially:**

We neglect Third World **languages, such as Arabic.**
We neglect non-European **languages, for example, Chinese.**

3 Even statements that each have a subject and a verb can turn into a fragment when they start with a **subordinator** (subordinating conjunction) like *if, when,* or *whereas* or a **relative pronoun** (*who, which,* or *that*).

FRAGMENT: Regular mail may take a week. *Whereas e-mail arrives the same day.*
EDITED: **Regular mail may take a week, whereas e-mail arrives the same day.**

Name _____

BUILDING THE HABIT

Study the following contrasting pairs. Read them over several times.

FRAGMENT:	Dorian was studying Hebrew. In Israel.
COMPLETE:	**Dorian was studying Hebrew in Israel.**
FRAGMENT:	Commuters spend hours on the road. Fighting the traffic.
COMPLETE:	**Commuters spend hours on the road fighting the traffic.**
FRAGMENT:	Europeans adore Jerry Lewis. The buck-toothed bozo.
COMPLETE:	**Europeans adore Jerry Lewis, the buck-toothed bozo.**
FRAGMENT:	My friends voted for losers. Most of the time.
COMPLETE:	**My friends voted for losers most of the time.**
FRAGMENT:	They were tracking condors. The West's largest birds.
COMPLETE:	**They were tracking condors, the West's largest birds.**
FRAGMENT:	Americans love gadgets. Like cellular phones.
COMPLETE:	**Americans love gadgets like cellular phones.**
FRAGMENT:	A media circus focused on O. J. Simpson. Acquitted in his first trial.
COMPLETE:	**A media circus focused on O. J. Simpson, acquitted in his first trial.**
FRAGMENT:	We read "The Lottery." A story about a typical small town.
COMPLETE:	**We read "The Lottery," a story about a typical small town.**
FRAGMENT:	The campers watched the sun. Rising over the top of Mt. Hood.
COMPLETE:	**The campers watched the sun, rising over the top of Mt. Hood.**
FRAGMENT:	Lady Diana died in a car crash in Paris. Mourned by millions.
COMPLETE:	**Lady Diana died in a car crash in Paris, mourned by millions.**

EDITING PRACTICE

Check each of the following. If there is a sentence fragment, rewrite the italicized part. If punctuation is right as it is, write *ok*.

1 Some fans had followed *the Grateful Dead. From concert to concert.*

_____

2 Moviegoers loved *Rambo. A superman in combat boots.*

_____

3 We finally found *the jeep. The thief had abandoned it.*

_____

4 She talked to the *other students. Preparing for the same test.*

_____

5 The place was a *ghost town. Most stores were empty.*

_____

6 The lecturer was *Clarence Thomas. The Supreme Court Justice.*

_____

7 The founder's nephew became *president. Nobody was surprised.*

_____

8 The book was a biography of *Robert Kennedy. Assassinated in Los Angeles.*

_____

9 They exercised *daily. With no visible results.*

_____

10 The agency found jobs for *workers. Displaced by downsizing.*

_____

11 The book featured early American *civilizations, such as the Aztec empire.*

_____

12 Wolves are back in wilderness *areas. For example, Yellowstone Park.*

_____

13 A young Asian architecture student designed the *Vietnam Wall. One of the great war monuments of all time.*

_____

14 Part-timers replaced *full-time faculty. Especially in two-year colleges.*

_____

15 Georgia did not require guns to be *licensed. In spite of massacres by gun-owning citizens.*

_____

CAPSULE RULE   Know how to punctuate two paired statements (semicolon
or comma?)

The safe punctuation between two complete separate statements is the **period.** However,
you may want to show that two statements are closely related. They go together. Use a **semicolon** (and start the second statement lower case).

> PERIOD: Fall came early. The leaves were turning yellow.
> SEMICOLON: **Fall came early; the leaves were turning yellow.**

1   Avoid two major editing problems with paired statements. A pair of statements *held together loosely* only by a comma is a **comma splice.**

> SPLICED: Eight people voted for *the motion, two* voted against it.
> EDITED: **Eight people voted for the motion; two voted against it.**

A pair of statements run together with *no punctuation* to separate them is a **fused sentence**.

> FUSED: The teenagers spent too much time *shopping they* often bought unneeded things.
> EDITED: **The teenagers spent too much time shopping; they often bought unneeded things.**

2   Use a semicolon when you pair two complete statements without any grammatical link.
(You are simply putting them next to each other.) There is an important *exception*: Use a
comma if you use a **coordinator** (coordinating conjunction) to show the connection.
The most common coordinators are **and** and **but**. The complete list is **and, but, so, for,
or, nor,** and **yet.**

> COMMA: Men are from Mars, **and** women are from Venus.
> The bond issue was passed, **but** the stadium was never built.
> The offer had expired, **so** the check was returned.

3   Use a semicolon if a **connecting adverb** shows the logical connection (for instance, point
and objection, or cause and effect; connecting adverbs are also called *adverbial conjunctions*). A partial list includes **however, therefore, moreover, nevertheless, besides, indeed,** and **in fact.** An optional comma (or optional commas) may separate these logical
links from the rest of the second statement.

> SEMICOLON: Workers expect pay raises and health benefits; **therefore,** factories install
> robots instead.
> The airwaves belonged to the public; **however,** Congress made them private property.

BACKUP EXPLANATION

In the paired statements that need the semicolon, each statement has its own subject and
verb. When such a statement becomes part of a larger combined sentence, we call it a **clause.**
Semicolons link **independent clauses**—statements that could easily be unhooked again and
become separate sentences.

TWO CLAUSES: The **blues** (SUBJECT) **came** (VERB) from the South; **it** (SUBJECT) **crossed** (VERB) the color line.

Do not use a comma with *and* or *but* when these words link only two words or phrases: They left the South **and went north.**

PROBLEM SPOTTER

Explain what the problem was in each pair and how it was solved.

NO: The door to the cabin was locked, the windows were open.
YES: **The door to the cabin was locked; the windows were open.**
NO: Pesticides kill insects herbicides kill weeds.
YES: **Pesticides kill insects; herbicides kill weeds.**
NO: The software was not compatible, we returned it.
YES: **The software was not compatible, so we returned it.**
NO: The alarm went off however we did not find a problem.
YES: **The alarm went off; however, we did not find a problem.**
NO: Genetic research is expensive government support is often necessary.
YES: **Genetic research is expensive; therefore, government support is often necessary.**

INSTANT REVIEW

In the space to the right of each sentence, put *S* if the sentence is punctuated right. Put *CS* if the sentence is a comma splice. Put *FS* if the sentence is a fused sentence.

1   Manuel was a gourmet cook; he refused to eat at McDonald's. _____

2   You must apologize she is angry about what you said. _____

3   You should speak to your lawyer, he will know how to handle the problem. _____

4   The crash caused a crisis of confidence; however, the success of the next mission restored confidence. _____

5   A professional-looking resume is very important it represents you. _____

6   Workers' earnings stayed low, many worked two jobs. _____

7   The laws limit the power of trusts, for they can force competition out of business. _____

8   Marcia's friends had free tickets they were unable to use them. _____

9   Her line is always busy, you should not call her during office hours. _____

10   We have not eliminated racial prejudice, we must keep trying. _____

FINER POINTS

■ Connecting adverbs (**however, therefore, nevertheless**) can shift to later in the second statement. The semicolon stays put.

DELAYED LINK: Workers want benefits; managers, **therefore,** prefer robots.
People hate taxes; the government collects them, **nevertheless.**

■ The additional commas with these words are left out in much current and especially in journalistic writing:

OMITTED COMMAS: Workers join unions; managers **therefore** shift production overseas.

Name _____

EDITING PRACTICE

Insert a comma or a semicolon where needed in the blank spaces in the following sentences.

1   Few businesses will cash personal checks _____ so a credit card _____ becomes a necessity.

2   Keeping a pit bull was made illegal _____ many people _____ see this as a necessary safety precaution.

3   The area had been overbuilt _____ therefore, many buildings stood empty.

4   My cousin sells draperies from his home _____ and over the Internet.

5   Gail had excellent management skills _____ yet she never stayed _____ very long in one job.

6   It is illegal to copy software _____ violators are prosecuted.

7   Beauty contests are controversial _____ promoters stress talent and not looks.

8   Her new car was expensive _____ but its economical performance _____ made it a good buy.

9   Michigan has many lakes _____ and rivers _____ Arizona has very few.

10   Generosity was not one of her virtues _____ but she was not ever malicious _____ or vindictive.

11   You will hear from us again _____ we will call no later than Monday.

12   During the holidays, the poor are remembered _____ with gifts of food and clothing.

13   Springsteen was their favorite singer _____ yet they owned none of his records.

14   Government safeguards prevent some outright scams _____ but many people still invest in doubtful schemes.

15   Schools promote "Just Say No" programs _____ maybe someday we will have a drug-free America.

16   Boxing is a popular sport _____ but very dangerous.

17   There are different kinds of vegetarians _____ some eat chicken or fish.

18   Publicity had been extensive _____ the turnout was poor however.

19   Warning signs had been posted _____ trespassers entered nevertheless.

20   You have to send the coupon _____ or the offer will expire.

FINAL REVIEW

What should be the punctuation at the break in each sentence? After each sentence, put C (for comma), SC (for semicolon), or No (for no punctuation).

1   Black bears are common __ however, grizzlies have become rare.   _____

2   Some 60,000 Mormons arrived in Utah before the railroad __ many converts came on foot.   _____

3   He wore a crumpled T-shirt __ it said "Hard Rock Cafe."   _____

4   The law protected the spotted owl __ and other indicator species.   _____

5   A threatened indicator species sends a signal __ other wildlife is also in trouble.   _____

6   The family never threw food away __ they put all leftovers in the icebox.   _____

7   The neighbors were always locking the doors __ and barring the windows.   _____

8   Reforestation brings new growth __ but the old-growth trees took hundreds of years to grow.   _____

9   Air pollution is not confined to the big cities __ smog, in fact, plagues Missoula, Montana.   _____

10 There are two metal clips on each side __ these hold the tray.   _____

11 Riots against the draft broke out in 1863 __ almost a hundred registrants were killed.   _____

12 The funds were cut off __ so the building remained unfinished.   _____

13 We cannot ban all insecticides __ for insects would inherit the world.   _____

14 The bear ate everything __ but the canvas bag.   _____

15 The bridge was already closed __ yet cars kept driving up.   _____

16 We showed our passes __ the guard would not admit us, however.   _____

17 The author was a socialist __ the authorities therefore would not give him a visa.   _____

18 The U.S. cannot play police to the rest of the world __ nor should we try.   _____

19 Humor makes people smile __ sarcasm makes them wince.   _____

20 Each pack carries a warning __ people smoke nevertheless.   _____

CAPSULE RULE   Choose the right forms of regular verbs.

Choose the right form of everyday regular verbs. Check the words you use when you talk about what people do or what happens. For instance, should it be **enter?** Should it be **enters?** Should it be **entered?** (You **enter** new data; your coworker **enters** new data; you **entered** other data yesterday.)

1   Use the plain or **unmarked** form of a verb for most present action:

UNMARKED PRESENT: I **exercise** daily. You **exercise** too little. All my friends **exercise** every day. Average Americans **do** not exercise enough.

2   Use the special *-s* ending for *one* person or thing, with present action—one third party, with action now (**third person singular**):

THIRD PERSON: He **exercises** every day. She **starts** the new job tomorrow. The bus **leaves** at eight. It often **arrives** late. Georgia **does** not require a license for gun owners.

3   Use the *-ed* (or *-d*) ending after any subject in the past (regardless of one or more—singular or plural):

PAST: Columbus **entered** the figures in the ship's log. Spanish missionaries **traveled** up the Royal Highway. The Maya **constructed** magnificent pyramids. The Spaniards **destroyed** the Aztec capital.

4   Use the form with *-ed/-d* also after forms of *have (has, had)*. These often point to the recent past (The shuttle **has reentered** the atmosphere). Often they point to the more distant past (The rocket **had lifted** off). The special kinds of past signaled by verbs with *have, has,* or *had* are called the **perfect** tenses.

RECENT PAST: The race **has started.** The contestants **have checked** in. The judges **have announced** a decision. The jury **has reached** a verdict.

DISTANT PAST: Ticket sales **had started.** The quarterback **had signed** a new contract. The FBI **had interviewed** the suspect.

5   Use the form with *-ed/-d* also after forms of *be* (including *is, are, was, will be, has been*). Use this form when the focus is not on what someone did (**active**) but on what was done (**passive**).

PASSIVE: The suspect **was cleared.** Violators **will be reported.** The search **has been discontinued.**

BACKUP EXPLANATION

■   Watch how verbs show time, or **tenses.** Verbs show a difference in time: It **snows** (now); it **snowed** (in the past); it **had snowed** (in the more distant past); it **will snow** (maybe tomorrow). For most English verbs, use the *-ed/-d* ending to show the change from present to past.

■   When talking about the **present** (action now), switch to the form with *-s* if you are talking about one single person or thing—one single third party (**third person**): my brother exercises—he **exercises**; my sister **exercises**—she **exercises**; the platoon (as a group) **exercises**—it **exercises**.

■ Do not use the *-ed* form after *do, does,* or *did.*

    NO: My roommate *did not exercised.*
    YES: **My roommate did not exercise.**

FINER POINTS

Watch for changes in spelling: apply-appl**ies**-appl**ied**; defy-def**ies**-def**ied**; plan-plans-plan**n**ed; commit-commits-commi**tt**ed, occur-occurs-occu**rr**ed, prefer-prefers-prefe**rr**ed.

INSTANT REVIEW

Each of the following sets puts a regular verb through its paces. In the blank spaces, fill in, first, the plain form or *-s* form as appropriate for the present. Then fill in the right form for the past. Then fill in *don't* or *doesn't* as appropriate.

1 I always *walk* to school. My sister also _____ to school. My father _____ to school in his day. My younger brothers _____ not walk school.

2 Each morning my brothers *start* to complain. My younger brother's car never _____ on a cold day. I _____ it for him yesterday. It's not my fault if his car _____ start.

3 My friends *work* during the summer. My best friend now _____ at night. Last summer, she _____ at a gas station. She _____ work there anymore.

4 Americans *protest* against injustices. Minorities _____ against inequality. The colonists _____ against unfair taxation. Some people _____ protest against anything.

5 Arguments *divide* families. The Mississippi _____ the country. The bandits _____ the loot. Some businesses _____ divide the profits fairly.

6 Americans love to *organize* things. Churches _____ picnics. The unions _____ workers. Some writers _____organize their thoughts.

7 Many Americans *investigate* their fellow citizens. Big corporations _____ job applicants. Last year Congress _____ big corporations. My college _____ investigate students.

8 Many workers *complain* about their jobs. My cousin always _____ about working conditions. Before his accident, he always _____ about insurance payments. He _____ complain anymore.

Name _____

PROBLEM SPOTTER

What was the problem in the original sentence? How was it resolved?

NO: Many pioneer families perish in the desert.
YES: **Many pioneer families perished in the desert.**
NO: Marcia collect beer mugs.
YES: **Marcia collects beer mugs.**
NO: Before they voted, they examine the evidence.
YES: **Before they voted, they examined the evidence.**
NO: The company had develop educational software.
YES: **The company had developed educational software.**
NO: Usually this type of bear don't hibernate.
YES: **Usually this type of bear doesn't hibernate.**

EDITING PRACTICE

Enter the number of the right choice after the sentence.

1 The new CEO always 1)talk/2)talks in glowing terms.   _____

2 Last year, the government 1)ban/2)banned several pesticides.   _____

3 Some people never 1)share/2)shares their good fortune with anyone.   _____

4 Last month, the family 1)announce/2)announced the engagement.   _____

5 Many teachers 1)doesn't/2)don't speak another language.   _____

6 My cousin always 1)sympathize/2)sympathizes with those in trouble.   _____

7 This morning, a detective 1)question/2)questioned the neighbors.   _____

8 Our country 1)doesn't/2)don't recognize their new government.   _____

9 People laid off 1)appreciate/2)appreciates advance warning.   _____

10 This week, the county fair 1)close/2)closes its doors.   _____

11 The company had 1)market/2)marketed fake apple juice.   _____

12 Athletes were being 1)test/2)tested for the use of steroids.   _____

13 After the indictment, the evangelist 1)resign/2)resigned.   _____

14 Publishers 1)advance/2)advances large sums for sensational bestsellers. _____

15 Many immigrants had completely 1)assimilate/2)assimilated.   _____

INSTANT REWRITE

A   All sentences in the following passage use the plain or **unmarked** form of the verb. Change all sentences to one person only (*third person present*).

EXAMPLE: New planes carry 700 people. **A new plane carries 700 people.**

Today's travelers love speed. High-speed trains travel at unsafe speed. Experts investigate crashes. Motorists ignore stop signs. Excess speeds kill.

_____

_____

_____

_____

_____

_____

_____

B All sentences in following passage use verbs in the present tense. Change all sentences to the past (**simple past**).

EXAMPLE: Airlines reduce leg room. **Airlines reduced leg room.**

Airline travel deteriorates. Executives calculate profit margins. Recorded messages replace live agents. Lines lengthen at check-in counters. One airline saves on peanuts.

_____

_____

_____

_____

_____

_____

_____

C All sentences in the following passage use the plain form of the verb after helping verbs like *may* or *will*. Change all sentences to the **distant past**, using *had*.

EXAMPLE: Congress may abolish the draft. **Congress had abolished the draft.**

The army will change. Volunteers will replace draftees. Women may train as pilots. Allies may coordinate operations. The Pentagon may develop high-tech weapons.

_____

_____

_____

_____

_____

_____

_____

CAPSULE RULE Choose the right forms of irregular verbs.

We call **irregular verbs** irregular because they do things differently. Irregular verbs do not simply add *-d* or *-ed* for the past. The word itself changes: **buy** (now)/**bought** (then); **write** (in the present)/**wrote** (in the past); **eat** (today)/**ate** (yesterday). In addition, most irregular verbs have a *third* form for use after *have* (*has, had*) to show recent past (I **have written** to them) or more distant past (I **had** already **written** it off).

■ Reviewing irregular verbs, you will often be looking at sets of three:

IRREGULAR: Learning a language **takes** time. The bus **took** us to the station. The illness **had taken** its toll.

IRREGULAR: The holiday **falls** on a Monday. The stock market index **fell**. Real estate price **had fallen**.

The combined forms using *have* (or *has* and *had*) are called the **perfect** forms. They often tell us about something recently completed or still important: They both **have chosen** their new partners. Or they tell us about something in the more distant past (before other things that happened in the past): We **pleaded** with them, but they **had** already **chosen** sides.

■ The same third form that appears after *have* also often appears after *be* and its many variations (*am, is are, was, were, has been*). Forms like **was chosen** or **had been sent** tell us not who did what (**active**) but what was done (**passive**).

PASSIVE: A new chair **is chosen** each year. The article **was written** anonymously. The contractor **will be taken** to court. The contract **had been broken.**

Use the right forms of irregular verbs for present, for past, and for use after *have* and *be:* I **see** (now). I **saw** (then). I **have seen** it (before now). I **was seen** (by someone else).

■ Whether used alone or as part of the main verb, the verb **be** can be a headache for writers used to a regional or down-home kind of English. *Be* has more different forms than any other English verb: I *am*, he or she *is*, they *are* (in the present); he or she *was*, we and they *were* (in the past); she *has been* absent, they *have been* here (for the perfect tenses). Watch especially for **singular** (*is, was*) and **plural** (*are, were*):

ONE THIRD PARTY (OR THING): The passport **is** valid. The speaker **was** late.

ALL OTHER: You **were** missed. They **are** suspects in the case. The newcomers **were** not welcomed.

BACKUP EXPLANATION

Many common verbs continue patterns for showing differences in time that go back hundreds of years. Group together irregular verbs that follow a similar pattern. Read the sets in each group over several times. Pay special attention to boldfaced forms. These are the **standard** forms and may be different from nonstandard forms you hear in some nonstandard or regional varieties of English.

GROUP 1: SWIM-SWAM-SWUM begin-**began**-have begun
sing-sang-have sung
drink-**drank**-have drunk
sink-**sank**-have sunk

GROUP 2:	BLOW-BLEW-BLOWN	fly-flew-have flown
		know-**knew**-have known (not *knowed*)
		grow-**grew**-have grown (not *growed*)
		throw-**threw**-have thrown (not *throwed*)

GROUP 3:	SPEAK-SPOKE-SPOKEN	break-broke-have **broken**
		freeze-froze-have **frozen**
		choose-chose-have chosen

GROUP 4:	Other -n or -en words	draw-drew-have drawn
		eat-**ate**-have **eaten**
		see-saw-have seen
		tear-tore-have **torn** (not *have tore*)
		drive-drove-have driven
		fall-fell-have fallen
		take-took-have **taken** (not *have took*)
		write-wrote-have **written**

GROUP 5:	Same for past and after *have*	bend-bent-have bent
		deal-dealt-have dealt
		lead-led-have led
		burst-**burst**-have **burst** (not *bursted*)
		dig-dug-have dug
		send-sent-have sent

GROUP 6:	One of a kind	do-did-done
		go-went-have **gone** (not *had went*)
		run-**ran**-have run
		come-**came**-have come

PROBLEM SPOTTER

What was the problem in each pair? How was it corrected?

NO: The police had went to the wrong address.
YES: **The police had gone to the wrong address.**
NO: Everybody in our town knowed everybody else.
YES: **Everybody in our town knew everybody else.**
NO: Most of the townspeople was recent immigrants.
YES: **Most of the townspeople were recent immigrants.**
NO: The ship had tore loose from its moorings.
YES: **The ship had torn loose from its moorings.**
NO: She had drove the road many times.
YES: **She had driven the road many times.**

FINER POINTS

Distinguish between **lie (lay, have lain)** and **lay (laid, have laid)**.

- The verb **lie** does not have an object; we just **lie** in the sun or **lie** in the shade (present). Priceless artifacts **lay** in King Tut's tomb (past). They **had lain** there for centuries. More examples for **lie:** Leaves now **lie** on the ground; patients were **lying** in their beds; I have to **lie** down.
- The verb **lay** is different. It has an object; we **lay** something—we **lay** tile, we **lay** bricks, we **lay** mines. In the past, we **laid** down the law or **laid** a rumor to rest.

Name _____

INSTANT REVIEW

For each of the following sets of sentences, fill in the missing forms of the same verb: -*s* form (third person, present singular); past form; and a form that follows *have* or *be*.

1 Many companies *send* their executives overseas. Fujitsu often _____ its American

   executives to Tokyo. Last winter, IBM _____ executives to Japan to study management

   styles. Many Japanese firms have _____ their executives to America.

2 Young people *wear* clothes that make a statement. A young person with money _____

   designer jeans. One year, everyone _____ pants with the designer's name on the back

   pocket. My cousin Leroy has never _____ anything stylish in his life.

3 Many teenagers *go* to the mall. Her mother now _____ to work in the evening.

   Hemingway _____ to live in Cuba. Shakespeare had _____ to the local

   grammar school.

4 Today's students *know* few of the classics. He _____ the poem by heart. Her great-

   grandfather _____ Mark Twain. We had _____ each other in

   high school.

5 Few students *take* Japanese. Learning a language _____ time. My high school friends

   _____ Spanish lessons. She had _____ our advice to heart.

EDITING PRACTICE

Write the numbers of the right choices in the blank spaces after the sentences.

1 At the earliest Olympics, athletes already 1)throwed/2)threw   _____

   the discus and 3)run/4)ran set distances.   _____

2 They 1)drove/2)driven from San Francisco to Los Angeles   _____

   and had 3)ate/4)eaten only Mexican food on the way.   _____

3 They 1)knew/2)known each other in college and   _____

   have 3)wrote/4)written regularly since.   _____

4 The letter had 1)fell/2)fallen from the mailbox and   _____

   someone had 3)tore/4)torn open the envelope.   _____

5 She had 1)wrote/2)written a letter of resignation after the   _____

committee 3)choose/4)chose a competing plan.   _____

6 Many swimmers 1)was/2)were in the water when   _____

the shark 3)swam/4)swum toward shore.   _____

7 Last year, bitter cold 1)come/2)came in November, and   _____

the lake had already 3)froze/4)frozen over.   _____

8 The climbers had already 1)went/2)gone ahead   _____

and had 3)took/4)taken most of the equipment with them.   _____

9 After we had been 1)drove/2)driven to the mansion,   _____

we were 3)lead/4)led into the library.   _____

10 Rumors 1)began/2)begun to spread that the ship   _____

had been 3)sunk/4)sank.   _____

CAPSULE RULE **Find the true subject of a sentence and make the verb agree with it.**

Nouns are the words we use to put labels on everything in the world around us. The two most basic sentence parts are often, first, a noun that brings something into focus and becomes the **subject** of the sentence. Then a verb makes a statement about it, often putting it in motion: **Planes** (Subject) **fly** (Verb). **Carpenters** (Subject) **build. Mechanics** (Subject) **repair** (Verb) cars. Most of the nouns we use as subjects have different forms for one at a time (**singular**) and several (**plural**):

SINGULAR AND PLURAL: one **applicant**/both **applicants**, one **plane**/several **planes**, one **institution**/ several **institutions**, one **woman**/several **women**, one **child**/many **children**

Often the form of the verb also changes as the subject changes from one to more than one:

SINGULAR AND PLURAL: one **works**/both **work**; one **does** the work/several **do** the work; one **is waiting**/many **are waiting**; one **was** ready/several **were** ready; one **has resigned**/they **have** all **resigned**

- **Agreement** is the choice of matching forms for subject and verb. Subject and verb agree when they are both singular or both plural.

SINGULAR: The **bus/stops** here. A **siren/was** wailing.
PLURAL: The **buses/stop** here. **Sirens/were** wailing.

Often the part of the verb that changes is the **helping verb**—a form of *have* or of *be*:

SINGULAR: The **package/has arrived.** A **virus/is attacking** computer files. The **concert/has been canceled.**
PLURAL: The **packages/have arrived.** **Viruses/are attacking** computer files. The **concerts/have been canceled.**

- Watch for agreement problems when the subject does not come right before the verb:

NO: The cost of the new prisons *are enormous.* (What's enormous?)
YES: **The cost** of the new prisons **is enormous.** (The cost is.)
NO: Arresting crack dealers *strain* police resources. (What's the strain?)
YES: **Arresting** crack dealers **strains** police resources. (Arresting them does)
NO: There *was* always people loitering outside. (Who was?)
YES: There **were** always **people** loitering outside. (People were.)

BACKUP EXPLANATION

Agreement requires matching forms of the subject and the verb. Subject and verb should be both singular: A bird/**sings** (we are clearly talking about one only). Or they should both plural: Birds/**sing** (we are clearly talking about more than one). Agreement problems occur (1) when subject and verb are separated or (2) when the subject is not clearly singular or plural.

- Ignore material that comes like a wedge between subject and verb:

SINGULAR: **Respect** (for our political leaders) **has declined.**
PLURAL: **Many voters** (supporting our candidate) **were disappointed.**

- In *there is/there are* sentences, look for the **postponed** subject—a subject that comes *after* the verb:

  SINGULAR: There **was little hope** for the survivors.
  PLURAL: There **were few survivors** of the crash.

- **And** often joins two subjects and makes the combined subject plural. **Or** may give us a choice of two singular subjects.

  PLURAL: The computer **and** the fax machine **have speeded** up our work.
  (the two together **have**)
  SINGULAR: A dirt bike **or** a dune buggy **chews** up the terrain.
  (either one **does** damage)

- Treat *each, either, neither,* and words like *everybody* and *nobody* as singulars. They may seem to point to more than one, but use them as if you were looking at the people involved *one at a time.*

  SINGULAR: **Each** of these options **has** serious drawbacks.
  Everybody on the staff **was updating** a résumé.

- Words ending in *-ing* may be singular or plural:

  SINGULAR: **Running** every day **keeps** him healthy. (**one** activity)
  PLURAL: Several **meetings** a day **keep** her running. (**several** activities)

PROBLEM SPOTTER

What was the problem in each of the following sentences? How has it been corrected?

NO: An ad in these small local newspapers produce results.
YES: **An ad in these small local newspapers produces results.**
NO: Inside the large envelope was several old photographs.
YES: **Inside the large envelope were several old photographs.**
NO: Each of the sisters are successful in their profession.
YES: **Each of the sisters is successful in her profession.**
NO: Close to the village, there is a monastery, a chapel, and a cemetery.
YES: **Close to the village, there are a monastery, a chapel, and a cemetery.**
NO: Carrot juice and seaweed has replaced beer and steak.
YES: **Carrot juice and seaweed have replaced beer and steak.**

FINER POINTS

- Know *unusual* plurals: one **crisis**/several **crises**, one **criterion**/several **criteria**, one unusual **phenomenon**/several unusual **phenomena**, one **medium** of communication/several of the **media**.

- If necessary, carry agreement through to sentence parts *other* than the verb. Study **extended agreement** in examples like the following:

  ILLOGICAL: Many advertisers now beam their messages at *women*
  who are *a wife, mother, and executive* at the same time.
  LOGICAL: Many advertisers now beam their messages at **women**
  who are **wives, mothers, and executives** at the same time.

- Check agreement after *one of those who:*

  PLURAL: I am not one of **those who believe** in vigilante action.
  (But there are *many* who believe in it.)
  SINGULAR: She is the **only one** of those women **who exercises** regularly.
  (Only *she* exercises.)

Name _____

INSTANT REVIEW

Put a check mark if the verb agrees with the subject.

The Losing Game of Politics

1 The political attitudes of college students *ranges* from apathy to enthusiasm.   _____

2 Running for minor local offices *costs* thousands of dollars.   _____

3 A race for senator or governor *requires* huge funds.   _____

4 Each of the candidates *make* wild promises.   _____

5 The qualifications of a candidate *is* almost impossible to evaluate.   _____

6 The media cannot accommodate every candidate who *is* asking for equal time.   _____

7 A loser or someone behind in the polls often *blame* the press.   _____

8 Victory in a political campaign *takes* time and money.   _____

9 A candidate without ample funds *have* little chance to reach the voters.   _____

10 There *is* often huge unpaid debts at the end of a campaign.   _____

EDITING PRACTICE

Which form is needed to make the subject and verb agree? Enter the number of the right choice.

1 The work of independent filmmakers often 1)goes/2)go unnoticed because of insufficient publicity.   _____

2 There 1)is/2)are always dozens of children playing in the park.   _____

3 Recycling bottles and aluminum cans 1)has/2)have become easy.   _____

4 The salary differential between men and women 1)was/2)were narrowing only slightly.   _____

5 The true charisma of a first-rate candidate 1)becomes/2)become a boon to a political party.   _____

6 Computer-simulated dissection of frogs or other small animals 1)has/2)have become an option in some science classes.   _____

7 In the dossier 1)was/2)were photographs of student protesters.   _____

8 Wearing the right clothes and being seen at the right parties 1)was/2)were top priorities at their school.   _____

9 Boosters in the Midwest 1)was/2)were building cities like Milwaukee and Cincinnati.   _____

10 The brutality of video games 1)mirrors/2)mirror the violence of our society.   _____

11 The work of brilliant modern artists often 1)has/2)have been neglected because people want the big names.   _____

12 A chance to travel and a congenial environment 1)was/2)were as important to her as the salary. _____

13 We worked all day with toxic substances, but there 1)was/2)were only inadequate safeguards for the employees. _____

14 There 1)was/2)were several planes backed up because of the ice. _____

15 The automated factory and global competition 1)has/2)have killed the demand for unskilled labor. _____

16 When a bear in our national parks 1)attacks/2)attack humans, the rangers relocate the animal. _____

17 The number of students in business courses 1)has/2)have exploded in recent years. _____

18 The existence of coed dorms 1)was/2)were news to our parents. _____

19 Either the supervisor or one of her assistants 1)has/2)have to stay in the office to handle emergencies. _____

20 The Dutch, from the richest to the poorest, 1)spares/2)spare nothing to make their houses clean and comfortable. _____

21 On the wall of the library 1)hangs/2)hang several paintings by lesser known American artists. _____

22 The misunderstandings caused by ignorance of foreign cultures 1)contributes/2)contribute to friction between nations. _____

23 The anniversary of the student revolt 1)reminds/2)remind us that students are often the first to demand political change. _____

24 The students in my dorm 1)prefers/2)prefer to study alone, in total silence. _____

25 My own childhood and several years of caring for my younger sisters 1)has/2)have helped me to understand young children. _____

CAPSULE RULE **Make your pronouns point clearly to what they stand for or replace.**

Pronouns often take the place of something mentioned earlier. If they stand for something else, make clear what it is. **He** may stand for *the governor;* **she** may stand for *the senator;* **they** may stand for *the reporters.* What "came before" is the **antecedent.** It should be clear what each pronoun is pointing to or replacing.

1 Do not let a pronoun point to *more than one* possible antecedent. Pronouns with an unintended double meaning are **ambiguous.**

AMBIGUOUS:	When the *President* honored the *poet,* we took a picture of *him.*
	(of whom, the President—or the poet?)
CLEAR:	We took pictures of the **poet** when the **President** honored **him.**
ALSO CLEAR:	We took pictures of the **President** when **he** honored the **poet.**

2 Avoid the **vague** use of *this* and *which.* Specify what the pronoun stands for:

AMBIGUOUS:	The pilot had *turned the plane around* because of *bad weather,* but the passengers were not aware of *this.*
	(of the weather? of the pilot's decision?)
CLEAR:	The pilot had **turned the plane around** because of **bad weather,** but the passengers were not aware of **this decision.**

3 Spell out **implied** antecedents. Fill in who *they* are in expressions like "In North Dakota *they* grow mostly wheat." (**The farmers** in North Dakota grow mostly wheat.) Specify what *you* really stands for in expressions like "First-class travel shows *you* are an important person" (refers only to passengers who can afford the ticket—not you and me).

INFORMAL:	In military academies, *they* maintain strict discipline.
	(who are they?)
SPECIFIED:	In military academies, **the staff** maintains strict discipline.
INFORMAL:	In the regular army, drill sergeants tormented *you.*
SPECIFIED:	In the regular army, drill sergeants tormented the **recruits.**

4 Make pronouns **agree** with their antecedents. An **it** should point back to a singular. A **they** should point back to a plural:

CONFUSING:	*Abortions* should not be banned because *it* is often required for medical reasons.
CLEAR:	**Abortions** should not be banned because **they** are often required for medical reasons.

BACKUP EXPLANATION

When you edit for pronoun reference, you ask: Who is *he* in this sentence? Who is *she?* What does the *it* or the *this* point back to?

■ Editing for pronoun reference often means finding the true "point of reference":

CONFUSED:	My sister is an *engineer,* but I'm not really interested in *it.*
	(what's *it?*)
CLEAR:	My sister's field is **engineering,** but I'm not really interested in it.

CONFUSED:	Her cousin had worked on a *river boat* during the summer, but in the winter *it* usually froze over.
CLEAR:	Her cousin had worked on **a river boat** during the summer, but in the winter **the river** usually froze over.

■ Check for everyday **informal plural pronouns** after reference to a typical person or to everyone in a group. (*Everybody* got on *their* bikes. *Nobody* sent in *their* checks.) Grammar books used to require the singular *he* (or *his*) in such situations, but not all bikers are male. Nonsexist language requires a **double pronoun: Everybody** got on **his or her** bike. **Nobody** sent in **his or her** check. When several uses of double pronouns like **he or she, his or her, himself and herself** would make a sentence awkward, try converting the whole sentence to the plural:

INFORMAL:	*A person* can never be too careful about *their* use of language.
NONSEXIST:	**A person** can never be too careful about **his or her** use of language.
ALL PLURAL:	**People** can never be too careful about **their** use of language.

INFORMAL:	*Everybody* on the team did *their* best.
NONSEXIST:	**Everybody** on the team did **his or her** best.
ALL PLURAL:	**All members** of the team did **their** best.

PROBLEM SPOTTER

What was the problem in each of the following sentences? How has it been resolved?

NO:	Martha moved in with her cousin, though she knows we dislike her.
YES:	**Though Martha knows we dislike her cousin, Martha moved in with her anyway.**
NO:	A patient may panic when they hear the diagnosis.
YES:	**Patients may panic when they hear the diagnosis.**
NO:	In New York, they have humid summers.
YES:	**New Yorkers have humid summers.**
NO:	We always saw movies that horrified you.
YES:	**We always saw movies that horrified us.**
NO:	Each student must hand in their homework on time.
YES:	**All students must hand in their homework on time.**

INSTANT REVIEW

Put a check mark if pronoun reference is satisfactory.

1   Each person runs differently, depending on their body size.   _____

2   Good advice and practice can help debaters improve their style.   _____

3   The average individual respects the wishes of the group because they hate to be
    considered odd.   _____

4   An artist may be extremely intelligent but unable to express it in verbal form.   _____

5   Prisons are run by undertrained and underpaid individuals, not to mention that they
    have a bad reputation.   _____

6   Many voters know little about Central America, which makes it difficult for the President
    to gain popular support for his policies.   _____

7   A uniformed guard may look official, but often he or she works for a private company.   _____

8   We believe that someone's religion is his or her own business.   _____

9   A boy was shot by an officer mistaking his toy gun for a real weapon.   _____

10 People must learn to have faith in themselves.   _____

Name _____

EDITING PRACTICE

Check pronoun reference. Enter the number of the right choice.

1   Every sports announcer makes 1)his or her/2)his share of mistakes.   _____

2   The groundkeepers watered the field twice a week, but 1)it/2)the water did not penetrate deeply enough.   _____

3   Tourists visit the mission churches that 1)they/2)the authorities have beautifully restored.   _____

4   A new officer is not hired unless 1)he or she/2)he passes a standard test.   _____

5   The mayor wanted to invite the governor, but 1)his/2)the mayor's handlers advised against it.   _____

6   A maverick does not just follow the party line of 1)his/2)his or her party.   _____

7   When Barbara Smythe became mayor, critics attacked 1)her/2)his or her use of funds.   _____

8   When Camille Paglia attacked Hillary Clinton, many sympathized with 1)her/2)the First Lady.   _____

9   When a poet dies, you may learn more than you want to know about 1)his/2)his or her private life.   _____

10   Everyone on the women's soccer team did 1)their/2)her best.   _____

11   If travelers fit a drug dealer's profile, customs agents will search 1)you/2)them carefully.   _____

12   Clinging to the Brahma bulls, the riders hung on as 1)they/2)the animals arched their strong backs.   _____

13   The staff went on strike, and management locked the doors of the station. 1)This/2)This lockout infuriated many listeners.   _____

14   At political fundraisers, 1)they/2)the organizers collect huge sums of money.   _____

15   The couple operated a pet hospital, but 1)they/2)the animals became too much trouble.   _____

16   If parents objected to their children's religious instruction, 1)they/2)the children used to be excused.   _____

17   If a child was from an Asian country, 1)they/2)he or she could not become a citizen.   _____

18   The judge ruled against the nativity scene on city property; the city council disapproved of 1)this/2)this decision.   _____

19   The instructor provided no background for the readings, 1)which/2) which lack of help made the course hard for most of us.   _____

20   The wife and the sister-in-law did not get along because of 1)her/2)the wife's informal lifestyle.   _____

INSTANT REWRITE

Solve the problems with pronoun reference in the following paragraph by converting all of the sentences to all plural. Compare your own rewrite with those prepared by your classmates.

EXAMPLE: *A politician* today receives a substantial part of *their* campaign contributions from an HMO. (shift to informal plural pronoun)

Politicians today receive substantial parts of their campaign contributions from HMOs. (all plural)

PARAGRAPH FOR REWRITE

The typical wage earner today is concerned about health care for their family. Often the doctor can no longer make his own decisions about his patients' needs. An accountant at an HMO decides on the basis of his company's guidelines. A patient is discharged from his hospital without his doctor's approval. When a woman has a difficult birth, you may be sent home early against your doctor's recommendations. The nurse may know better, but her knowledge of her patients doesn't count.

_____

_____

_____

_____

_____

_____

_____

_____

_____

_____

_____

_____

_____

_____

_____

_____

_____

_____

CAPSULE RULE   Use the right pronoun form for subject or object.

Many common pronouns change their form depending on where you use them in a sentence. Use the right pronoun form for the **subject** of a verb: **I** agreed, **he** refused, **she** has resigned, **we** collaborate, **they** pay the rent. Use the right pronoun form for the **object** of a verb: excuse **me**, ask **him**, support **her**, invited **us**, had ignored **them**. Use the object form also after a preposition— a word like *in, by, at, for, about, with, without, between,* or *among:* aimed at **us**, good for **them**, signed by **her**, all right with **me**.

SUBJECT	OBJECT	OBJECT OF A PREPOSITION
She introduced	**me**	to **him.**
I directed	**them**	to **her.**
He connected	**us**	with **them.**
They referred	**her**	to **us.**

In shortened sentences using *as* or *than* you may have to fill in a missing verb. You can then see whether a pronoun is used as subject or object:

SUBJECT: No one was as demanding as **she** (was). He was faster than **I** (was).
OBJECT: They admired him as much as (they did) **her.** They paid him more than (they paid) **me.**

BACKUP EXPLANATION

The pronouns that change from subject form to object form often point to persons, and we call them **personal pronouns.** The different subject and object forms are called **case** forms. The pronouns that have different case forms are **I/me, he/him, she/her, we/us,** and **they/them.** (**You** and **it** stay the same: **You** hired them. They hired **you.**)

■ Use the right form in **double subjects** (or compound subjects): **She and I** ran every morning (not *her and me* ran).

DOUBLE SUBJECT: **The supervisor and I** had a talk. (NOT *me and the supervisor*)
She and her friends had left. (NOT *her and her friends*)
He and the boss often disagreed. (NOT *him and the boss*)

Use the right forms also in **combined subjects** like **we students** or **we Americans:**

COMBINED: **We Americans** tend to be generous. (NOT *us Americans*)
Often **we youngsters** tire of the hard-luck stories of the older generation.
(NOT *us youngsters*)

■ Use the right form in **double objects** (or compound objects): The supervisor called **my colleague and me** back (NOT *my colleague and I*).

DOUBLE OBJECT: The picture showed **the manager and me.** (NOT *and I*)
We invited **her and her friends.** (NOT *she*)
We heard **him and the boss** arguing. (NOT *he*)

Use the right forms also in **combined objects** like **us students** or **us Americans:**

COMBINED: He always supported **us scouts.** (NOT *we scouts*)

■ Use the right form in **double objects** of prepositions—words like *with, for, by, without, about, around, in, at:* This is between **you and me** (NOT between *you and I*).

DOUBLE OBJECT: We have reserved space for **you and her**. (NOT *she*)
We had a meeting with **him and his manager**. (NOT *he*)

Use the right forms also in **combined objects** of prepositions:

COMBINED: They should send the data to **us stockholders**. (NOT *we*)

PROBLEM SPOTTER
NO: Me and the supervisor worked hand in hand.
YES: **The supervisor and I worked hand in hand.**
NO: Us scouts are always eager to help.
YES: **We scouts are always eager to help.**
NO: We scheduled her friend and she for an interview.
YES: **We scheduled her friend and her for an interview.**
NO: We have complimentary tickets for Jean and he.
YES: **We have complimentary tickets for Jean and him.**
NO: All this is strictly between you and I.
YES: **All this is strictly between you and me.**

INSTANT REVIEW
Change the following from the subject form to the object form:

he _____ they _____ she _____ I _____ we _____

Change the following from the object form to the subject form:

me _____ her _____ them _____ us _____ him _____

FINER POINTS
Who is the subject form. **Whom** is the object form. In questions, **who** asks a question about the subject. (**Who** is their backup quarterback?) **Whom** asks a question about an object. (**Whom** did the team cut to make room for him?)

1 Use **who** when you ask about, or point to, the subject of a verb: **Who** is active? **Who** cares? **Who** is being targeted? Often the *who* starts a second clause in the larger combined sentence:

SUBJECT: We want people **who** care. People **who** smoke are becoming less popular.

2 Use **whom** when you ask about, or point to, the object of a verb.

OBJECT: **Whom** did they appoint? (They appointed *him*.) He was the kind **whom** only a mother could love. (She loved *him*.)

Sometimes you can sidestep the *who/whom* dilemma altogether:

NO WHO/WHOM: He was the kind only a mother could love.

3 Use **whom** also when you ask about, or point to, the object of a preposition (with **whom?** for **whom?** by **whom?**).

OBJECT: With **whom** was he last seen? (With *her*.) I forget to **whom** the bill was sent. (It was sent to *him*.) She knows the brother from **whom** I am estranged. (I am estranged from *him*.)

4 When choosing between **who** and **whom**, disregard material that comes between a **who** and its verb:

SUBJECT: **Who** (would you say) **is** America's most famous athlete?
Who (do you think) **will win?**

Name _____

REVISION PRACTICE
Enter the right pronoun that should replace the wrong form used in the sentence.

1   I had some letters for she and her mother.   _____

2   The information should remain between you and I.   _____

3   My brother and me had no respect for our coworkers.   _____

4   Space visitors might smile at the technology us earthlings possess.   _____

5   They always invited the other neighbors and I.   _____

6   He persuaded my friends and I to buy the new computer.   _____

7   Congress ignores the feelings of we taxpayers.   _____

8   His father and him had gone on hunting trips.   _____

9   Two police officers were waiting for Sam and she.   _____

10 Bad luck had befallen he and his family.   _____

11 Her and the other workers never got along.   _____

12 Him and his dogs drove me crazy.   _____

13 Her and I applied for the same job.   _____

14 We need candidates who the voters trust.   _____

15 Whom do you think will win?   _____

PRONOUN CASE REVIEW
Enter the number of the right choice.

1 A teacher persuaded my friend and 1)I/2)me to study computer languages. _____

2 Lead in the air and asbestos in the walls concern you as much as 1)we/2)us. _____

3 Students realized that unregistered, unlicensed guns were a lethal menace to their teachers and 1)they/2)them. _____

4 There was a strong spirit of competition between her sisters and 1)she/2)her. _____

5 Marion spent a year teaching English to Japanese students and learned as much as 1)they/2)them. _____

6 The reporter asked him 1)who/2)whom his backers were but got no reply. _____

7 Strictly between you and 1)I/2)me, the forecast seems inflated. _____

8 Last year, 1)she/2)her and her coworker conducted a workshop in Oregon. _____

9 The police were looking for a man 1)who/2)whom fit the description. _____

10 The crew and 1)I/2)me were too careless to pay attention to the captain's warning. _____

11 Children with learning disabilities need therapists 1)who/2)whom they trust. _____

12 Other employers will make you a better offer than 1)they/2)them. _____

13 People need someone to 1)who/2)whom they can turn in time of need. _____

14 With 1)who/2)whom did you negotiate the contract? _____

15 Doris told her associates that she was just as objective as 1)they/2)them. _____

16 His interviewer had liked the other applicants better than 1)he/2)him. _____

17 He was the man 1)who/2)whom witnesses saw running away from the fire. _____

18 Nations around the world turn to 1)we/2)us Americans for help. _____

19 They liked Maria's qualifications but wanted someone with more experience than 1)she/2)her. _____

20 1)We/2)Us children of baby boomers will live in a different world. _____

CAPSULE RULE   Use the adverb form to tell us how (or when or where) something is done.

Both adjectives and adverbs bring additional details into a sentence. **Adjectives** modify nouns. They tell us which one or what kind: the **sad** song, an **easy** answer, a **careful** driver, a **frequent** flyer, a **considerable** gain. **Adverbs** modify verbs. They tell us how, when, and where something is done: speak **sadly**, driving **carefully**, returning **frequently**, having improved **considerably**.

1   When you have a choice, use the adverb form to modify a verb. Often you can change an adjective to an adverb by adding the -*ly* ending: **cheerful/cheerfully, careful/carefully, happy/happily, serious/seriously**.

   -ly: The **bright** star (which?) shone **brightly** (how?).
   -ly: The **cheerful** performer (what kind?) always smiled **cheerfully** (how?).
   -ly: The **terrible** events (which ones?) hurt the family **terribly** (how much?).

2   Know how to use the most common irregular adverb: **Good** people do things that are **good** (adjective), but we do something **well** (adverb). Things work **well** (how?); people speak a language **well** (how?); they look for a **well**-paying job (paying how?).

3   Use adverbs not just to modify verbs. Use them also to modify *another* modifier—an adjective or another adverb.

   ADVERB + ADJECTIVE: It was a **surprisingly beautiful** evening. (how beautiful?)
   ADVERB + ADVERB: You sang **admirably well**. (how well?)

4   Adverbs most often go with verbs to fill in the *how* of an action. However, adjectives instead of adverbs follow a special kind of verb. After **linking verbs**, adjectives answer the question: What is it like? Linking verbs work like an "equal" sign—they say "this is like that." Linking verbs include **be** (and its many forms, including **is, are, was, were, will be, has been**), **become, look**, and **feel**.

   ADJECTIVES: The customer was **furious**. The losses were **considerable**. The argument became **ridiculous**. The agent turned **hostile**. The soup smelled **delicious**. The pit bull looked **angry**.

BACKUP EXPLANATION

In informal everyday English, many adjectives do double duty as adverbs. In your writing, use distinctive adverb forms when you have a choice.

■   To show how something is done or how something operates, use the form with the added *-ly:*

   INFORMAL: The choir sang *beautiful*. The sisters educated us very *strict*.
   EDITED: The choir sang **beautifully**. The sisters educated us very **strictly**.

■   Avoid using *good* and *bad* as adverbs. Use **well** and **badly** instead.

   INFORMAL: Some animals don't hear *good*. (how?) We needed supplies *bad*. (how much?)
   EDITED: Some animals don't hear **well**. We needed supplies **badly**.

■ Avoid informal expressions like *real popular, awful expensive,* and *pretty good.* Use **very** in such combinations or a distinctive adverb like **really, fairly,** or **extremely.**

> **INFORMAL:** The dog was *pretty sick.* It was a *real boring* movie.
> **EDITED:** The dog was **very sick.** It was a **truly boring** movie.

PROBLEM SPOTTER

What was the problem in each of the following sentences? How was it resolved?

NO: The receptionist greeted us bright and cheerful.
YES: **The receptionist greeted us brightly and cheerfully.**
NO: The population had grown considerable.
YES: **The population had grown considerably.**
NO: This morning, the motor was running good.
YES: **This morning, the motor was running well.**
NO: She was always driving very careful.
YES: **She was always driving very carefully.**
NO: It was an awful expensive evening and real boring.
YES: **It was a very expensive evening and extremely boring.**

INSTANT REVIEW

Put a check mark after each sentence using the right adverb form.

1 He played the drums expertly.   ____

2 Daniel was real serious about his studies.   ____

3 The Internet was expanding incredibly fast.   ____

4 The officer opened the door very cautious.   ____

5 The politics of Central America have changed considerable.   ____

6 During the storm, everyone drove too fast.   ____

7 She swam effortlessly across the pool   ____

8 Everyone was afraid to tell them how bad we had done.   ____

9 The staff worked very diligent on the project.   ____

10 The senator acted extremely hopeful at the party.   ____

FINER POINTS

1 Not all words ending in *-ly* are adverbs, telling us how. Some exceptional words end in *-ly* and are not adverbs but adjectives. They tell us which one or what kind: a **friendly** talk, a **lonely** life, a **leisurely** drive, a **lovely** flower.

2 Not all adverbs are different from the corresponding adjective. For words like **fast, late, hard, much,** and **early,** the adjective and adverb are the same.

> **SAME FORM:** The **early** bird gets up **early.** The **late** riser gets up **late.** The **hard** assignments made us work **hard. Much** talk does not mean **much.**

3 Some special uses of adjective and adverb forms: We feel **bad** but act **badly;** we look **good** and are **well** (in good health).

4 Informal adverbs like *slow, quick,* and *loud* now often appear in writing. To be safe, you can change them to drive **slowly,** react **quickly,** speak **loudly.**

Name _____

REVISION PRACTICE
Enter the letter for the right choice.

1   Historically, American voters have not taken primary elections _____.
      a real serious   **b** very seriously   **c** very serious   _____

2   After winning the pie-eating contest, Jim was not feeling _____.
      a very well   **b** real good   **c** very good   _____

3   Greg played his horn so _____ that the neighbors complained.
      a frequent   **b** frequently   **c** very frequent   _____

4   Despite his _____ behavior, David had many friends.
      a pretty arrogant   **b** real arrogant   **c** extremely arrogant   _____

5   It was _____ for the office staff to adjust to the new supervisor.
      a awful hard   **b** extremely hard   **c** pretty hard   _____

6   The students did not know how _____ the new teacher was.
      a strictly   **b** strict   **c** real strict   _____

7   Students from their school were doing _____ in college.
      a real good   **b** very good   **c** very well   _____

8   The teacher spoke so _____ we had a hard time taking notes.
      a quickly   **b** quick   **c** rapid   _____

9   The crowd behaved _____ despite the heat.
      a fairly good   **b** really good   **c** fairly well   _____

10 The managers failed _____ to motivate their employees.
      a miserable   **b** miserably   **c** terrible   _____

11 His main point never became _____.
      a clear   **b** clearly   **c** real clear   _____

12 The new office manager was _____ unpleasant.
      a consistent   **b** consistently   **c** regular   _____

13 The retiring CEO spoke _____ about her future plans.
      a firmly   **b** firm   **c** real firm   _____

14 Few applicants performed _____ on this exam.
      a good   **b** well   **c** pretty good   _____

15 The quality control team inspected parts _____.
      a regular   **b** regularly   **c** real regular   _____

16 The bus driver had failed to stop _____.
      a deliberate   **b** deliberately   **c** very deliberate   _____

17 The survivors had become _____.
      a desperate   **b** desperately   **c** pretty desperate   _____

18 The company replaced defective software _____.

    a real reluctant   **b** very reluctant   **c** very reluctantly   _____

19 The older people spoke English _____.

    a surprising good   **b** surprising well   **c** surprisingly well   _____

20 Management dressed _____ at her company.

    a very casually   **b** real casual   **c** very casual   _____

SENTENCE PRACTICE

For each sentence, fill in five or six distinctive adverb forms that could complete the sentence. Compare your entries with those of your classmates.

EXAMPLE: We work out _____ , _____ , _____ , _____ , _____
          We work out **regularly, frequently, barely, strenuously, reluctantly, eagerly**

1 They continued the rescue efforts

_____

_____

_____

2 The athletes performed

_____

_____

_____

3 People dress

_____

_____

_____

4 Speakers may speak

_____

_____

_____

5 Voters may support a candidate

_____

_____

_____

CAPSULE RULE Make your modifiers point clearly to what they modify.

Modifiers bring additional details into the basic subject-verb sentence. They modify different things depending on where you place them: I asked **only my friend** for a loan (you asked nobody else). I asked my friend **for a loan only** (you did not ask for a gift).

When a modifier is **misplaced,** it seems to point in the wrong direction:

MISPLACED: *At age twelve, his father* bought him his first rifle.
(his father was twelve?)

EDITED: His father bought **him** his first rifle **at age twelve.**

When a modifier is left **dangling,** what it points to has been left out from the sentence.

DANGLING: *To play tennis properly,* the racket must be held firmly.
(Who plays?)

EDITED: **To play** tennis properly, **a player** must hold the racket firmly.

BACKUP EXPLANATION

Look for the different kinds of modifiers that might have to be placed with care. Check the following especially:

■ Check the position of **adverbs** like *only* and *almost:*

Riots **almost broke out** at every soccer game. (But they never quite did.)
Riots broke out at **almost every soccer game.** (They did frequently.)

■ Prepositional phrases (starting with words like *with, without, at,* or *by*) are often misplaced or left dangling:

MISPLACED: The manager looked at the packages *we had stacked with disgust.*
(stacked with disgust?)

EDITED: **The manager** looked **with disgust** at the packages we had stacked.

■ Modifiers may be **verbals**—parts of verbs or forms of verbs that are not being used as a complete verb in a sentence. Verbals are forms like *smiling, having smiled,* and *to smile* (**Smiling,** he opened the door) or *exhausting, exhausted,* and *being exhausted* (**Exhausted,** she left the field).

MISPLACED: *Buzzing around the room, I* finally killed the fly.
(You were buzzing around the room?)

EDITED: I finally killed the **fly buzzing around the room.**

MISPLACED: *Coming out of the shower, reporters* mobbed the quarterback.
(Who showered?)

EDITED: **Coming out of the shower, the quarterback** was mobbed by reporters.

PROBLEM SPOTTER

What was the problem in each sentence? How was it resolved?

NO: We pried open the door we had inadvertently locked with a screwdriver.
YES: **With a screwdriver, we pried open the door we had inadvertently locked.**

NO: At the age of nine, our relatives visited from Mexico.
YES: **When I was nine years old, our relatives visited from Mexico.**
NO: To obtain good grades, good study habits are essential.
YES: **To obtain good grades, a student has to develop good study habits.**
NO: The island had a museum for tourists with shrunken heads.
YES: **For tourists, the island had a museum with shrunken heads.**
NO: Dangling from a pair of tweezers, the youngster held a huge moth.
YES: **The youngster held a huge moth dangling from a pair of tweezers.**

INSTANT REVIEW

Check placement of modifiers. Put a check mark after each sentence that is satisfactory.

1 Being a normal youth, the safety lectures were boring.   _____

2 Hearing only impersonal voice mail, callers may get angry.   _____

3 Inspired by a century-old poem, the song celebrates Manhattan.   _____

4 When taking a bath, a radio should not be left close to the tub.   _____

5 The gunman fired at the officers pursuing him with an automatic weapon.   _____

6 Having grown up in Wyoming, my cousin never liked the big city.   _____

7 The painting was called the best ever painted by my art teacher.   _____

8 By glancing over the magazine rack in any drugstore, many are either men's magazines
   or women's magazines.   _____

9 Having eluded its keepers, the bear was captured the next day.   _____

10 Once big and costly, computers are becoming smaller and cheaper.   _____

FINER POINTS

A **squinting** modifier points in two directions at once.

SQUINTING: The police discovered *inadvertently* they had released the wrong suspect.
(discovered inadvertently—or released inadvertently?)
EDITED: The police **inadvertently discovered** they had released the wrong suspect.

Name _____

EDITING PRACTICE

Enter the letter for the better choice on the right.

1 The restaurant offers _____   _____
    a special meals for seniors that are inexpensive.
    b special meals that are inexpensive for seniors.

2 Homeless people _____   _____
    a collecting cans and bottles used to come to where I lived.
    b used to come to where I lived collecting cans and bottles.

3 To enter the mansion, _____   _____
    a the alarm had to be disconnected.
    b intruders had to disconnect the alarm.

4 Sharks are a danger   _____
    a when tourists swim in tropical waters.
    b when swimming in tropical waters.

5 Our group _____   _____
    a turned down the invitation to attend the ceremony with regret.
    b regretfully declined the invitation to attend the ceremony.

6 Speeding down the highway, _____   _____
    a an overturned rig blocked the road.
    b we came upon an overturned rig blocking the road.

7 To use software, _____   _____
    a customers have to read thick manuals.
    b reading the manuals is essential.

8 _____ my sister taught me to roller skate.   _____
    a Because I had very little coordination,
    b Having very little coordination,

9 Athletic scholarships should go _____   _____
    a equally to men and women with no strings attached.
    b to men and women equally with no strings attached.

10 The United States _____   _____
    a almost won every war it entered.
    b won almost every war it entered.

11 Reading about the train wreck later in the paper, _____   _____
    a three of the passengers were killed.
    b I learned three of the passengers were killed.

12 Funded by a special bond issue, _____   _____
    a the hospital was hailed as a success.
    b the media called the hospital a success.

13 To taste authentic, _____   _____
    a the cook should let the stew simmer for an hour.
    b the stew should simmer for an hour.

14 Dressed in colorful airy costumes, _____ ____

    a the critics were charmed by the dancers from Taiwan.

    b the dancers from Taiwan charmed the critics.

15 Some insecticides _____ ____

    a are still used on crops although suspected of being dangerous.

    b suspected of being dangerous are still used on crops.

INSTANT REWRITE

Rewrite the following passage to improve the position of modifiers. (*Hint:* You may want to make an adjustment in every sentence.)

In our society today, children may come to a new school with limited English proficiency. To be better prepared, parents should consider preschool or mentoring programs. Children come to mentors with a variety of problems. Learning a second language, the usual teachers and ordinary textbooks may not be enough. By criticizing the language of the home, children may be alienated from school. Even when raised in an English-speaking home, school may present new challenges. Talking to a fellow student, the conversation might be very informal. However, writing a paper, the teacher will look for a more formal kind of English.

CAPSULE RULE Straighten out confused or illogical sentences.

When a sentence seems confused, straighten out basic relationships by asking: "Who does what? What is being compared with what? What caused what?" Rewrite confused sentences like the following:

1   Check your sentences for unintentionally **duplicated** elements, especially words like *of* and *that:*

DUPLICATION:	We heard *that* because the station had been bombed *that* no trains would arrive. (only one *that* is needed)
EDITED:	We heard **that** because the station had been bombed no trains would arrive.
DUPLICATION:	The paintings were finally returned to the museums *from* which they had been looted *from.* (only one *from* is needed)
EDITED:	The paintings were finally returned to the museums **from** which they had been looted.

2   Don't confuse different ways of expressing the same idea. Check your sentences for **mixed construction.** In each of the following examples two possible ways of saying the same thing have become entangled:

RIGHT:	The course was canceled **because not enough people registered.**
ALSO RIGHT:	The course was canceled **because of insufficient registration.**
MIXED:	The course was canceled *because of not enough people registered.*

RIGHT:	The villagers showed us the new tractor **of which they were proud.**
ALSO RIGHT:	The villagers showed us the new tractor **that they were proud to have bought.**
MIXED:	The villagers showed us the new tractor *of which they were proud to have bought.*

3   Avoid excessive **shortcuts.** "We *were invited* but Jim *turned away*" should be "We **were** invited, but Jim **was** turned away." "*Faith and respect for* the American public" should be "**faith in** and **respect for** the American public." In the following sentences, also, too much has been left out:

SHORTCUT:	My grandparents *moved* to Hawaii and *have rarely visited* them. (who visited?)
COMPLETE:	My grandparents moved to Hawaii, and **I have rarely visited** them.
SHORTCUT:	Thousands *contracted* typhus but *did not reach* the city.
COMPLETE:	Thousands contracted typhus, but **it did not reach** the city.

BACKUP EXPLANATION

Study some common reasons why parts of a sentence might not fit together:

■   Make sure that what the **verb** says can logically apply to the subject of the sentence.

ILLOGICAL:	The *introduction* of the guest speaker *was introduced* by Dean Stile, chair of the committee. (what was introduced? not the introduction but the *guest speaker*)
EDITED:	The **guest speaker was introduced** by Dean Stile, chair of the committee.

Similarly, make sure that **linking verbs** (especially forms of *be: is, are, was, were, has been, will be*) join things that are logically equal.

ILLOGICAL: A *student* with a part-time job *is* a common cause of delays in graduation.
(a student is not a cause; the part-time job is)

EDITED: A student's **part-time job** is **a common cause** of delays in graduation.

Watch for an *is* or *was* that should lead to *what* something is—but instead leads to *when* something happens. Rewrite *is-when* sentences:

ILLOGICAL: An eclipse *is when* the moon obscures the sun.
EDITED: An eclipse **occurs when** the moon obscures the sun.

■ An **appositive** is a second noun that puts a label on the first: Frank Lloyd Wright, **the builder**; Margaret Thatcher, **the former prime minister.** Make sure that the label can logically apply to what it labels:

CONFUSED: There was only *one bid* for the building, *a Texas cattleman.*
(A cattleman is not a bid, and a bid is not a cattleman.)

EDITED: There was only **one bidder** for the building, **a Texas cattleman.**

■ Make sure you are comparing things that are comparable. Rewrite sentences with incomplete or **illogical comparisons**:

ILLOGICAL: A talk show host's *opinions* reach a wider audience than *a college professor.*
EDITED: A **talk show host's** opinions reach a wider audience than **a college professor's.**
(or **those of a college professor**)

Clarify three-cornered comparisons:

CONFUSED: We feared *the guards* more than *the inmates.*
CLEAR: We feared the guards more **than the inmates did.**
ALSO CLEAR: We feared the guards more **than we did the inmates.**

PROBLEM SPOTTER

What was the problem in each sentence? How has the problem been resolved?

NO: The price of these luxury apartments was incredibly expensive.
YES: **These luxury apartments were incredibly expensive.**
NO: In case of blackouts should be reported immediately.
YES: **Blackouts should be reported immediately.**
NO: Her previous job was a mail carrier.
YES: **She was previously employed as a mail carrier.**
NO: Her personality was unlike most other people I have known.
YES: **Her personality was unlike that of most other people I have known.**
NO: The cabin was destroyed by fire, of which they had always been afraid of.
YES: **The cabin was destroyed by fire, of which they had always been afraid.**

FINER POINTS

Some expressions common in everyday informal English will be considered incomplete or illogical when you use them in writing.

INCOMPLETE: Shareholders these days make *more money.*
(than what other group?)
COMPLETE: **Shareholders these days make more money than the workers.**

ILLOGICAL: *Just because* people make teasing remarks *does not mean* they don't like us.
(a cause is not a meaning)
EDITED: **That** people make teasing remarks **does not mean** they don't like us.

Name _____

INSTANT REVIEW

Put a check mark after each sentence that is satisfactory.

1 While we were in college, I admired Jerry's discipline and study skills and have continued in his professional life.   _____

2 The playwright told us that if we invited her she would come.   _____

3 The UN sent a peacekeeping force, an international contingent.   _____

4 In an era of dwindling resources, we will all have to give up conveniences to which we are used to.   _____

6 The author received angry letters, mostly members of the NRA.   _____

7 Much piecework is done by workers dissatisfied with repetitive tasks who are yearning for more interesting work.   _____

8 The public throughout supported the President more than the media did.   _____

9 A well-regulated militia is very different from a private arsenal of semiautomatic weapons.   _____

10 By cutting the number of jurors in half greatly reduces the time used in selecting a jury.   _____

EDITING PRACTICE

Enter the letter for the right choice.

1 Tran graduated from an American university in four years,   _____

   a of which he was very proud of.
   b an accomplishment of which he was very proud.

2 Andrew has contributed to many charities,   _____

   a and have used his name to solicit other contributors.
   b and they have used his name to solicit other contributors.

3 You have only   _____

   a one message, from a former employer.
   b one message, a former employer.

4 The patient was given an injection,   _____

   a and the instruments were made ready.
   b and the instruments made ready.

5 Her campaign for state senate failed   _____

   a because of not enough supporters contributed.
   b because not enough supporters contributed.

6 Only one vacancy was posted on the board,   _____

   a a position for a research engineer.
   b a research engineer.

7 Tolerance   _____

   a is when we respect other people's views.
   b means respecting other people's views.

8 _____ always crowded. _____

    a The attendance at these poetry readings is
    b These poetry readings are

9 The purpose of these vans _____

    a is to be all-purpose vehicles for the suburbs.
    b is designed to be all-purpose vehicles for the suburbs.

10 My typing is not as good as _____

    a that of an experienced secretary.
    b an experienced secretary.

11 Computer viruses were tracked down, _____

    a and security given a higher priority.
    b and security was given a higher priority.

12 Discipline, for me, _____

    a is a school with teachers in control.
    b requires a school with teachers in control.

13 Dedication meant that in spite of poor conditions _____

    a that teachers would do their best.
    b teachers would do their best.

14 We thought that Leroy's attitude was exactly _____

    a like that of other members of the fraternity crowd.
    b like other members of the fraternity crowd.

15 When I arrived at the store, the doors were still locked, _____

    a and had to turn on the lights.
    b and I had to turn on the lights.

16 Americans as a nation _____

    a are made up of dozens of foreign customs and cultures.
    b draw on dozens of foreign customs and cultures.

17 The reorganization of the company _____

    a was entrusted to a "turn-around" specialist.
    b was reorganized by a "turn-around" specialist.

18 The CEO rejected him _____

    a to be one of her assistants.
    b as one of her assistants.

19 A "dress for success" image _____

    a is created when women avoid an overly feminine appearance.
    b is when women avoid an overly feminine appearance.

20 _____ has to be reported to the police. _____

    a In case of an accident
    b An accident

CAPSULE RULE   Rewrite weak passives on the "who does what" model.

An **active** sentence focuses on the action in a sentence. It goes from the "doer" through the action to the target or result: Economy-minded **customers** (doer) **bought** (action) smaller **cars** (target). A **passive** sentence turns this perspective around and puts the target first. It then tell us what is happening to it. The original target (or object) becomes the subject of the new sentence. Smaller **cars** (original target) **were bought** (passive verb) by economy-minded **customers** (original "doer"). In the **short passive,** the original "doer" or agent is left out altogether: **Evolution** (original target) **was banned** (passive verb) in Kansas (sentence does not say by whom).

When you change active verbs to passive verbs, you use a form of *be* (*is, are, was, were, had been, will be,* and others). You then use the form of the main verb that also appears after *have* (as in *have* **bought**).

ACTIVE VERB: **can** no longer **ignore, are discriminating** against, **will select, has continued, had chosen, would have announced, is training**

PASSIVE VERB: **is** often **ignored, are discriminated** against, **was selected, will** not **be continued, has been chosen, had been previously announced, are being trained**

Weak passives get in the way of the reader who wants to know who does what. "An inquiry *is being conducted by* the mayor's office" is wordy and roundabout. "The mayor's office **is conducting** an inquiry" is more straightforward and direct. "Questions about tax money for public television *are being raised*"—by whom? (**Conservative politicians** regularly **raise** these questions.) Convert weak passives to stronger active sentences that clearly tell the reader who does what:

WEAK PASSIVE: The investigation *is being continued* by the police.
STRONGER ACTIVE: **The police is continuing** the investigation.
WEAK PASSIVE: The word-processing capability of personal computers *is seen by many teachers* as a revolutionary tool for writing.
STRONGER ACTIVE: **Many teachers see** the word-processing capability of personal computers as a revolutionary tool for writing.

BACKUP EXPLANATION

In the passive, the subject and the object have traded places. In an active sentence, the doer or instigator comes first. (**Americans** love **pets.**) In a passive sentence, the target or result comes first. (**Pets** are spoiled by **Americans.**) Passives in themselves are neither good nor bad. Many languages have them. The passive is the right choice when the target or result of an action seems more important than the performer. It puts the spotlight on the result, not the cause. The passive is also often appropriate when the doer or performer of an action is beside the point or hard to identify.

STRONG PASSIVE: Mandatory **jail sentences will be imposed** on drunk drivers.
       (The mandatory sentence is the main point.)
STRONG PASSIVE: In World War II, **millions of people were driven** from their homes.
       (That millions were displaced is the main point.)
STRONG PASSIVE: The last **condors were sighted** here in 1946.
       (The focus is on the condors.)

INSTANT REVIEW

Which of the following sentences are active? Which are passive? Enter A for active sentences, P for passive.

1 Many viewers have turned to cable television for better programs.   _____

2 The range of television transmission has been greatly extended by satellites.   _____

3 Today's entrepreneurs engineer mergers of megacompanies.   _____

4 According to the Kansas Board of Education, human beings have not evolved to a higher level from apes.   _____

5 Sandra Day O'Connor was appointed to the Supreme Court.   _____

6 American tourists have profited from favorable exchange rates for the dollar.   _____

7 The government eased regulations for commercial radio stations.   _____

8 Many banking transactions are now handled by computers.   _____

9 Inflation was brought under control in many countries of the West.   _____

10 European nations adopted a common currency.   _____

11 The negotiations were conducted with great secrecy.   _____

12 Plans for a Holocaust Memorial were being debated.   _____

13 Visitors place flowers and mementos at the Vietnam Wall.   _____

14 A memorial for female veterans was added to the monument.   _____

15 A Korean War memorial is the latest addition.   _____

PROBLEM SPOTTER

What was the problem in each of the following sentences? How was it resolved?

NO: Watching the passing ships is enjoyed by many.
YES: **Many people enjoy watching the passing ships.**
NO: Much study time has to be invested by the ambitious student.
YES: **Ambitious students have to invest much study time.**
NO: Pollution of the air, of the land, and of the seas has to be fought by all.
YES: **We all have to join in the fight against pollution of the air, of the land, and of the seas.**
NO: Inflation is identified as the main threat to continuing prosperity.
YES: **Conservative economists identify inflation as the main threat to continuing prosperity.**
NO: Alternative sources of energy have been experimented with by many nations.
YES: **Many nations have experimented with alternative sources of energy.**

Name _____

EDITING PRACTICE

In the edited more direct version of the following passive sentences, what is the missing active verb? Enter the missing verb.

1   Iran was accused by the United States of supporting terrorists.

The United States _____ Iran of supporting terrorists.

2   Action will be taken by local governments to help conserve water.

Local governments _____ action to help conserve water.

3   All student vehicles must be parked only in designated areas.

Students _____ their vehicles only in designated areas.

4   A motion had been made by a committee member to approve the report.

A committee member _____ a motion to approve the report.

5   As part of their duties, all gates and windows are regularly checked by the two security guards.

As part of their duties, the two security guards regularly _____ all gates and windows.

6   In the schools of China, much copying and memorization had been expected of students.

In the schools of China, teachers _____ much copying and memorization

of their students.

7   A new treaty covering fishing grounds was being negotiated by Canada and the U.S.

Canada and the U.S. _____ a new treaty covering fishing grounds.

8   If an invigorating and affordable sport is wanted, cross-country skiing is a perfect choice.

If people _____ an invigorating and inexpensive sport, cross-country skiing

is a perfect choice.

9   An explanation should have been offered by the conductor for the long delay.

The conductor _____ an explanation for the long delay.

10   Private cars had been banned at the prom by the school board, with buses provided.

The school board _____ private cars at the prom, with buses provided.

INSTANT REWRITE

Rewrite the following passage, changing all passive sentences to active.

EXAMPLE: Lives *are being risked by* protesters against logging companies.
Protesters against logging companies **are risking** their lives.

Rearguard actions against big new projects are often fought by nature lovers. In Great Britain, plans for a new freeway were contested by protesters. Challenges to the project had been overruled by the authorities. The endangered forest was loved by ecologists and nature lovers. Tree houses were constructed in the threatened trees. Supplies were hauled up by rope. Months were spent in the trees by dedicated activists. However, the logging machinery and the hardhats could not be stopped. One tree dweller was treed like a raccoon by a lumberjack with a chainsaw.

_____

_____

_____

_____

_____

_____

_____

_____

_____

_____

_____

_____

_____

_____

_____

_____

_____

_____

_____

_____

_____

CAPSULE RULE **Do not confuse your readers by shifts in perspective.**

1   Stay in the same timeframe. Do not jump suddenly from the past to the present. Stay in the past even if your story suddenly turns dramatic and vivid:

ALL PAST: We **trudged** along when a bear **came** (not *comes*) around the bend.
ALL PAST: The crowd **surged**, and suddenly the gate **gave** (not *gives*) way.

Distinguish between the past and the more distant past. If necessary, show that something had happened earlier—before other events in the past:

DISTANT PAST: Her husband **said** that he **had been** (not *was*) a confirmed bachelor.

2   Watch out for the generalized *you*. Avoid the **you** that does not specifically refer to **you, the reader**, but points to no one in particular: "*You* had to be eighteen to enlist." In particular, do not shift from *I* or *we* to *you*, or from *they* to *you*, or from *a person* to *you* when you are still talking about the same person.

SAME PERSON: **We** had nothing illegal, but the officers searched **us** (not *you*) anyway.
SAME PERSON: **I** hate streets where **I** (not *you*) cannot walk after dark.
SAME PERSON: **A person** has to stay calm when **she is** (not *you are*) unjustly accused.

3   Avoid unnecessary shifts from the active voice (she **does** something) to the passive (it **is done** by her). Try not to shift to the passive (something is done by someone) when the same person is still active in the sentence.

SAME PERSON ACTIVE: The settlers **invaded** the forest and **cut down** many trees.
(NOT: and many trees *were cut down*)
SAME PERSON ACTIVE: The dentist **had gone** to work and **had pulled** several teeth.
(NOT: *and several teeth had been pulled*)

BACKUP EXPLANATION

To be **consistent** means to follow through when you have adopted one way of looking at the timeframe, at people, or at what they do.

■   When you are telling a story, you ask yourself: Am I telling this as if it were happening now (**present**)? Or am I reporting it as something that happened then (**past**)? And am I showing that other events had taken place earlier (**distant past**)?

■   Use *you* (**second person**) only when you mean "you the reader." Do not shift to the general *you* if you started by using *I* or *we* (**first person**) or *they* (**third person**). Do not shift to the general *you* when you started with an expression like *a person* or if you actually identified the people involved.

■   Many languages have one set of verb forms for something people do: I **invited** them (**active**). They have another set for something that is done by them or to them: I **was invited** (**passive**). When the same person is still active, or when the same causes are still at work, do not confuse the reader by shifting to the passive.

PROBLEM SPOTTER

What was the problem in each of the following sentences? How was it resolved?

NO: As I walk by the shop, the owner stared at me.
YES: **As I walked by the shop, the owner stared at me.**
NO: When a woman faces an abortion, you realize how serious it is.
YES: **When a woman faces an abortion, she realizes how serious it is.**
NO: I sprained an ankle, and a doctor had to be consulted.
YES: **I sprained an ankle and had to consult a doctor.**
NO: Women are overcoming prejudice and proving ourselves.
YES: **Women are overcoming prejudice and proving themselves.**
NO: The lecturer criticized management, but the workers were also attacked.
YES: **The lecturer criticized management but also attacked the workers.**

INSTANT REVIEW

Which of the following sentences are consistent, without confusing shifts? Write yes or no.

1 The rain fell for days; then suddenly the sun shines.   _____

2 People do not appreciate good things if bad luck has never been experienced.   _____

3 The singer started, and a hush fell over the crowd.   _____

4 A person should not give up because others put you down.   _____

5 Though he was rich and famous, he died in poverty.   _____

6 We had waited for days when help finally arrived.   _____

7 She saw the pedestrian, and the brakes were slammed on.   _____

8 Many people stop when the street musicians perform.   _____

9 I saw the sheriff in the rear view mirror and head for the embankment. _____

10 You need to proofread your writing not just for misspelled words but also for
    computer glitches.   _____

FINER POINTS

Be consistent when dealing with *possibilities*. Are they *real* possibilities? Deal with them as a factual possibility (probable) or as a remote if (more unlikely).

SHIFT: If they **come** to this country, the government **would offer** them asylum.
FACTUAL: If they **come** to this country, the government **will offer** them asylum.
IFFY: If they **came** to this country, the government **would offer** them asylum.

SHIFT: If terrorists **threaten** to use a nuclear weapon, what **would we do**?
FACTUAL: If terrorists **threaten** to use a nuclear weapon, what **will we do**?
IFFY: If terrorists **threatened** to use a nuclear weapon, what **would we do**?

Name _____

REVISION PRACTICE

For each of the following sentences, put a check mark next to the right choice.

1   The instructor told us to save papers

    a   on your floppy disks. _____

    b   on our floppy disks. _____

2   Taking everything we need,

    a   we launch the rafts. _____

    b   we launched the rafts. _____

3   We lighted the wood and before long

    a   had a fire blazing. _____

    b   have a fire blazing. _____

4   Students from minority backgrounds should do more

    a   to have your voices heard. _____

    b   to have their voices heard. _____

5   The governor went through the budget

    a   and many items were blue-penciled. _____

    b   and blue-penciled many items. _____

6   We were leaving the building

    a   when the ground starts shaking. _____

    b   when the ground started shaking. _____

7   The celebrity endorsing the product

    a   had been an astronaut walking on the moon. _____

    b   was an astronaut walking on the moon. _____

8   Many in the crowd grew restless, and

    a   the speakers were booed. _____

    b   they booed the speakers. _____

9   "Cramming" is the practice of charging phone customers

    a   for services you did not order. _____

    b   for services they did not order. _____

10   "Slamming" means switching a customer's phone carrier

    a   without the customer's knowledge. _____

    b   without your knowledge. _____

11 A pit bull had broken loose, and

    a it mauled a child. _____

    b a child was mauled. _____

12 He cut himself off from his friends

    a and his work was neglected. _____

    b and neglected his work. _____

13 The National Fraud Information Center tracks frauds,

    a and it ranked sweepstakes frauds Number One. _____

    b and sweepstakes frauds were ranked Number One. _____

14 The con artists declaring us million-dollar winners

    a think you are a total idiot. _____

    b think we are total idiots. _____

15 The loudmouth talk show host goaded the contestants

    a until one contestant hits his mother-in-law. _____

    b until one contestant hit his mother-in-law. _____

CAPSULE RULE When you duplicate sentence elements, stay with sentence parts of the same kind.

Links like *and* or *but* often set up a pattern: **jogging** and **walking**; **red, white,** and **blue**; **Democrat, Republican,** or **Independent**; **television, the movies,** and **the rest** of the media. Once the pattern is set up, readers expect you to use the same or similar sentence parts—sentence parts that are **parallel** or of the same kind. When something snaps out of the pattern, parallel structure breaks down. Avoid **faulty parallelism:** Sentence parts joined by *and*, *or*, or sometimes *but* should fit into the same grammatical category: **body and soul;** (two nouns); **swear and affirm** (two verbs); **kicking and screaming** (two verbals); **poor but proud** (two adjectives).

NOT PARALLEL:	The uncle was *antisocial and a miser* besides.
	(adjective + noun)
PARALLEL:	The uncle was **antisocial and stingy** besides.
	(adjective + adjective)
NOT PARALLEL:	A commercial must manage *to attract attention* and also *being remembered*.
PARALLEL:	A commercial must manage **to attract** attention and also **to be remembered.**
	(two *to* forms, or infinitives)

BACKUP EXPLANATION

Check parallel sentence structure in situations like the following especially:

■ Avoid linking a *noun with an adjective* as modifiers of another noun:

NOT PARALLEL:	The schools must satisfy both *personal and society* needs.
PARALLEL:	The schools must satisfy both **personal and social** needs.
	(two adjectives that both tell us what kind of needs)

■ Check for parallel structure when using **paired connectives:** *either . . . or, neither . . . nor, not only . . . but also,* and *whether . . . or.* (They **not only met** us at the station **but also offered** us a place to sleep—two verbs both telling the reader what someone did.)

NOT PARALLEL:	The refugees debated whether *to return* or *should they wait*.
PARALLEL:	The refugees debated **whether to return or to wait.**

■ Avoid faulty parallelism in a **series** of three or more elements. A series should be three or more sentence parts *of the same kind:*

NOT PARALLEL:	They liked *to harass* shopkeepers, *overturn* garbage cans, and *other bullying tactics*.
PARALLEL:	They liked **to harass** shopkeepers, **overturn** garbage cans, and **bully** fellow citizens.

PROBLEM SPOTTER

What was the problem in each of the following sentences? How was it resolved?

NO:	They spoke to a lawyer who lived in L.A. and knowing O. J. Simpson.
YES:	**They spoke to a lawyer who lived in L.A. and knew O. J. Simpson.**

NO:	They preferred to live in the country and commuting to the city.
YES:	**They preferred to live in the country and commute to the city.**
NO:	Most weekends, she was either in the library or working at the computer.
YES:	**Most weekends, she was either studying in the library or working at the computer.**
NO:	Computer programs can now check student papers for spelling, awkward sentences, and to avoid the use of sexist language.
YES:	**Computer programs can now check student papers for spelling, awkward sentences, and sexist language.**
NO:	The story focuses on whether dinosaurs can be brought back to life and keeping them confined on an island.
YES:	**The story focuses on whether dinosaurs can be brought back to life and kept confined on an island.**

INSTANT REVIEW

Check the following sentences for parallel structure. Put a check mark on the right for each sentence that is satisfactory.

1 My job included sweeping out the store, hosing down the sidewalk, and restocking the shelves.   _____

2 In computer science, we studied using programing languages and how to build a website.   _____

3 The dresses they sell are stylish, different, and at a good price.   _____

4 More and more movies are including scenes of mayhem, torture, and rape.   _____

5 Men in home economics classes were learning how to cook, clean, and take care of their families' needs.   _____

6 The counselor said that I should rest and not to get excited or upset.   _____

7 Draft picks were asked whether they were used to travel and did they mind being away from their families.   _____

8 The owners told the anxious buyer that they wouldn't change their minds and not to worry. _____

9 TV ratings help parents who want to monitor what their children watch or to block some programs altogether.   _____

10 Foreign student may have trouble understanding the local customs and getting to know Americans.   _____

FINER POINTS

The elements in a faulty series may not really be parallel in *meaning*. You may then decide to break up the series altogether.

NOT PARALLEL:	The new manager was *brash, inexperienced, and an MBA from Harvard.*
BETTER:	The new manager, an MBA from Harvard, was **brash and inexperienced.**

Name _____

EDITING PRACTICE

Rewrite the italicized part of each sentence to make it parallel.

1 The new arrivals were dirty, *undernourished, and regarding everyone with suspicion.*

_____

2 Our visitor liked to repair things around the house and *his own cooking.*

_____

3 The vacationers went on long hikes, rowed around the lake, or *just leisure time.*

_____

4 Government agents not only put dissidents under surveillance but also *tapping their phones.*

_____

5 The dean asked about my grades and *would I return next year.*

_____

6 Immigration officials screened immigrants for diseases and *did they have proper documentation.*

_____

7 Directors were looking for stars who were beautiful, *intelligent, and for younger audiences.*

_____

8 The best way to fight juvenile crime is not to impose harsher sentences but *by restoring old-fashioned discipline in the home.*

_____

9 The inner city is starved of good jobs, viable businesses, *and no cultural life to speak of.*

_____

10 Social workers hear about illnesses, housing problems, and *how domestic arguments get started.*

_____

11 The manual explained how to build a gun cabinet, how to make a bookcase, and *other kinds of furniture.*

_____

12 When I was a member of the team, everyone made friendly conversation and *being invited to many parties.*

_____

13 Many Americans now object to *both ethnic and race labels.*

_____

14 Fans love college basketball because any team can win and *a fine display of teamwork.*

_____

15 My friends were always going off to jog in the park or *a game of volleyball.*

_____

16 The personnel director asked me to fill in an application form and *would I leave my number.*

_____

17 Yosemite is a park with spectacular scenery and *which has half-tame bears.*

_____

18 Employees had a choice of either signing the loyalty oath or *their contract was terminated.*

_____

19 The tenant returned to pay the rent and *also picking up some belongings.*

_____

20 The accused had neither been seen at the scene of the crime nor *any identification of his car by the neighbors.*

_____

CAPSULE RULE   Use the standard English of school, office, and the media.

Standard English is like the national currency. It is good everywhere. While many Americans are comfortable with the rural English, Southern English, or inner-city English they grew up with, on official or public occasions they shift gears. They speak and write the standard American English that is the national currency of communication. Some of the most noticeable differences between standard English and nonstandard speech show in the use of verbs. Which of these will you have to work on?

1   Use the standard forms of English verbs. Speakers of nonstandard English need to work on the so-called **irregular verbs.** These often have *three different forms* of the main verb—depending on how they are used in the sentence. You need to know sets of three like the following: **take** (now), **took** (past), have **taken** (recent past); **choose** (now), **chose** (past), have **chosen; know** (now), **knew** (past), have **known; go** (now), **went** (past), have **gone.**

PRESENT:	Many Americans **know** Spanish.
PLAIN PAST:	The voters **chose** Clinton.
RECENT PAST:	A new millennium **has begun.**
DISTANT PAST:	The stage coach **had become** obsolete.

"Shakespeare **wrote** *Romeo and Juliet*" shows the ordinary past (often past and done with). The third form usually follows **have** (or **has** or **had**). "Almost everyone connected with the White House **has written** a book" shows recent past (people are still reading these). "The former vice-president **had written** a book about the family" shows distant past (no one reads it anymore). The forms with *have* (*has, had*) are grouped together as the **perfect** tenses (or timeframes) of a verb.

BUILDING THE HABIT

Review the following sets of three especially. Read them over several times, one group at a time.

begin-began-have **begun**
drink-drank-have **drunk**
go-went-have **gone** (not *have went)*
eat-ate-have **eaten**

know-knew-have **known** (not *knowed)*
grow-grew-have **grown** (not *growed)*
throw-threw-have **thrown** (not *throwed)*

break-broke-have **broken** (not *have broke)*
freeze-froze-have **frozen** (not *have froze)*
choose-chose-have **chosen** (not *have chose)*

see-saw-have **seen**
tear-tore-have **torn** (not *have tore)*
take-took-have **taken** (not *have took)*
write-wrote-have **written** (not *have wrote)*

In such sets of tense forms, sometimes one of the forms is used twice—sometimes three times:

lead (present)-**led** (past)-have **led**
run (present)-**ran** (past)-have **run**
come (present)-**came** (past)-have **come**
burst-burst-have **burst** (not *bursted*)

2   The same form that follows *have* often follows a form of *be* (like ***is, are, was, were, will be, has been***). It then makes up the **passive**. The passive highlights not who *does* what but what *was done* by whom.

> PASSIVE: Families **were torn** apart. (not *were tore*)
> Children **were taken** from their mothers. (not *were took*)
> The fish **had been frozen** while still on the ship. (not *had been froze*)

3   In the **present** (things happening now), check for the *-s* ending for "one third party, present tense." Use the form with *-s* after *he, she,* or *it* (**third person singular**): he **agrees**, she **dissents**, it **matters**. Use it also after words that you could replace with *he, she,* or *it.* (**The train connects** major cities. **It connects** Paris and Berlin.) Several people *do* things together; sometimes a newcomer **does** or **doesn't** join in.

BUILDING THE HABIT

Read the examples of standard forms over several times. Go back to them after a time.

> NONSTANDARD: He *work* at the new plant. She *live* in a loft downtown. It *rain* almost every day. It *don't* matter.
>
> STANDARD: He **works** at the new plant. **His sister** also **works** there. **She works** the night shift. **The** new alarm **system works** well. **It works** better than we expected. It **doesn't** always work.
>
> STANDARD: The typical **student** here **lives** on campus. **He or she lives** in a dorm or coop. **The** typical **instructor** also **lives** close by.
>
> STANDARD: **Our group organizes** meetings. The congregation **organizes** field trips. It **organizes** discussion groups. The radical caucus **organizes** protests. It **doesn't** meet often.

4   Watch for forms of *be*. The verb *be* has more different forms and uses than any other English verb. Watch especially for **singular** and **plural**: *is/are, was/were.* (The form after *you* is the same for singular and plural: *you are/you were*—never *you is* or *you was.*)

> PRESENT: I **am**, he or she **is**, it **is** (singular)
> we **are**, you **are**, they **are** (plural)
> PAST: I **was**, he or she **was**, it **was** (singular)
> we and they **were** (plural)
> PERFECT: she **has been** absent (singular)
> they **have been** here (plural)

BUILDING THE HABIT

Read the examples of standard forms over several times. Go back to them after a time.

> NONSTANDARD: You *was* not on the list. The regulations *is* always being changed. The rescuers *was* exhausted. You *was* always busy.
>
> STANDARD: I **was** accepted but you **were** not. We **were** invited but she **was** not. The regulations **are** fine as they **are**. The rescuers **were** exhausted. They **were** too tired to talk. We **were** free, but you **were** always busy.

Name _____

PROBLEM SPOTTER

What was the problem in each pair? How was it corrected?

NO: The police had went to the wrong address.
YES: **The police had gone to the wrong address.**
NO: Everybody in our town knowed everybody else.
YES: **Everybody in our town knew everybody else.**
NO: Most of the townspeople was recent immigrants.
YES: **Most of the townspeople were recent immigrants.**
NO: The ship had tore loose from its moorings.
YES: **The ship had torn loose from its moorings.**
NO: Her parents is still living in the same house.
YES: **Her parents are still living in the same house.**

EDITING PRACTICE

Choose the right verb. Enter its number on the right.

Let the Games Begin

1   At the earliest Olympics, Greek athletes already 1)throwed/2)threw the discus.   _____

2   They 1)run/2)ran set distances.   _____

3   At recent Olympic Games, athletes 1)have broke/2)have broken many records.   _____

4   The typical spectator 1)doesn't/2)don't just admire the big stars.   _____

5   Audiences cheer athletes who 1)was/2)were injured but finish anyway.   _____

6   Tickets for soccer games now 1)is/2)are in big demand.   _____

7   The Olympic Committee has 1)chose/2)chosen spectacular sites for the winter Games.   _____

8   The police has often 1)taken/2)took extensive security precautions.   _____

9   Charges of steroid use have 1)tore/2)torn the Olympic community apart.   _____

10   Several winners 1)was/2)were asked to return medals.   _____

11   In Utah the newspapers 1)went/2)gone public with charges of bribery and corruption.   _____

12   For big corporations, the Games 1)is/2)are big business.   _____

13   Only a rare gold medal winner 1)don't/2)doesn't sign up to promote running shoes or athletic equipment.   _____

14   Even so the ordinary fan 1)watch/2)watches the Games for the thrill of competition.   _____

15   Athletes from around the globe 1)competes/2)compete peacefully every four years.   _____

CAPSULE RULE **Edit for widely used features of nonstandard English.**

Widely heard features of nonstandard English don't interfere with communication. The meaning comes through when the blues singer sings "Nobody knows you when *you down and out*." However, nonstandard ways of saying things allow people to make judgments (right or wrong) about your educational level, occupational status, or social background.

Edit your writing for features that to your readers will sound like neighborhood English, rural English, blue-collar English, or regional English rather than the standard English of school and office. If you hear any of the following regularly, make sure not to carry them over into your writing:

1 Check for missing forms of *have* (*has, had*). Check for missing forms of *be* (*is, are, was, were*). Read the standard forms in the following sets over several times:

MISSING *have:*	She *done* her job. He *beaten* the odds. He *been looking* for work. The polls *been closed* for hours.
STANDARD:	She **has done** her job. He **had beaten** the odds. He **has been looking** for work. The polls **have been closed** for hours.
MISSING *be:*	He from the South. They truly sorry. Chicago a huge city. They trying to recruit new members.
STANDARD:	He **is** from the South. They **are** truly sorry. Chicago **is** a huge city. They **are** trying to recruit new members.

2 Use the standard forms of pronouns. The standard **pointing** pronouns (demonstrative pronouns) are **this** and **these**, **that** and **those**: We cannot win at **this** time and in **these** circumstances (not *this here* time). Help us track **those** funds (not *them* funds).

NONSTANDARD:	*this here* car, *that there* road, *them* tickets
STANDARD:	**this car, that road, those tickets**

The *-self* **pronouns** (reflexive pronouns) point back: **He** did it **himself; they** did it **themselves; we** tried it **ourselves.**

NONSTANDARD:	*hisself, themself* and *theirself, ourself*
STANDARD:	**himself, themselves, ourselves**

3 Avoid **double negatives**, which say no twice. To avoid a double negative, you can often change a second *no* to a word like *any.*

NONSTANDARD:	*Nobody* there did *nothing* to help us. We *never* did *nothing* to offend him. *Didn't nobody* care.
STANDARD:	**Nobody** there did **anything** to help us. We **never** did **anything** to offend him. We did **nothing** to offend him. **Nobody** cared.

4 Use *an* instead of *a* before a vowel: **an athlete**, not *a athlete;* **an outing**, not *a outing.*

▪ Vowels are *a, e, i, o,* and *u.* Use the *an* before a vowel: **an eye** for **an eye, an earful, an A, an accident, an informed** reader, **an unimportant** point. But use *an* before *u* only if it sounds like the *u* in *up*, not like "you": **an upturn**, but *a U-turn.*

■ Use *a* before a consonant: *a* desk, *a* launch, *a* hotel, *a* beehive. Go by what you hear, not by what you see spelled. It's **an F** (pronounced *eff*) and **an honest** man (pronounced *onnest*). But it's *a university* (pronounced with a *you* sound).

> **NONSTANDARD:** *a* ear, *a* accident, *a* athlete, *a* automobile
> **STANDARD:**   **an ear, an accident, an athlete, an automobile**

5 Standard English does without **double reference**. Omit the personal pronoun that immediately follows a noun and seems to duplicate it : My **adviser told** me I was wrong (not My *adviser he* told me I was wrong). The other **witness said** the opposite (not The other *witness she* said the opposite).

6 Check for the missing plural *-s* that should show more than one for nouns:

> **NONSTANDARD:**   The in-laws lived about *sixty mile* from here.
> **STANDARD:**   The in-laws lived about **sixty miles** from here.

PROBLEM SPOTTER

What was the problem in each of the following sentences? How was it resolved?

NO: The counselor didn't do nothing about the problem.
YES: **The counselor didn't do anything about the problem.**
NO: She never paid no attention to parking tickets.
YES: **She never paid any attention to parking tickets.**
NO: Gerald was repairing his car hisself.
YES: **Gerald was repairing his car himself.**
NO: It was a honor to meet the Secretary of State.
YES: **It was an honor to meet the Secretary of State.**
NO: Them politicians in Washington are cut off from the people.
YES: **Those politicians in Washington are cut off from the people.**

BUILDING THE HABIT

Let the right forms sink in. Read them over several times.

1 It is **an honor** to meet such **an important** person.

2 Getting **an M.A.** takes less time than getting **a Ph.D.**

3 The owners reserved **those rooms** for **themselves.**

4 All week we **never** saw **any** police officers.

5 Joan **never** believed in **anything** or **anybody.**

6 He received **an A** on the final but **a B** in the course.

7 Her alibi **didn't** fool **anyone.**

8 **An athlete** cannot always have **an outstanding** season.

9 **This camp** did **not** offer **any** modern conveniences.

10 **The owner himself** told us to keep the money for **ourselves.**

Name _____

INSTANT REVIEW

Choose the standard form. Enter the number for the standard form on the right.

1   Shouting at people never solves 1)nothing/2)anything.   _____

2   The group didn't have the money to pay 1)them/2)those lawyers.   _____

3   Gary was 1)a/2)an eight-year-old with tired old eyes.   _____

4   The positively worded announcement didn't fool 1)anybody/2)nobody.   _____

5   The governor 1)himself/2)hisself answered our letter.   _____

6   The coalition represented 1)a/2)an broad spectrum of interests.   _____

7   The witness had himself worked in 1)a/2)an asbestos plant.   _____

8   The earthquake 1)done/2)had done little damage.   _____

9   The ordinance made it easier for 1)them/2)those developers.   _____

10 The plainclothes officers never identified 1)themselves/2)themself.   _____

11 The loan office has moved to 1)that there/2)that building.   _____

12 The candidates 1)being/2)are being interviewed tomorrow.   _____

13 Usually all the lines 1)busy/2)are busy.   _____

14 The new 1)doctor she/2)doctor talks little with the patients.   _____

15 The climbers 1)had been/2)been warned about avalanches.   _____

EDITING PRACTICE

Make each of the following sentences standard English by changing one word. Write the changed word in the blank to the right of each sentence.

1 The driver never forgave hisself for killing that deer. _____

2 A unnerving howl awakened the campers. _____

3 Many industries never did nothing to protect the environment. _____

4 The plane was scheduled to leave in less than a hour. _____

5 The settlers never did anything to protect theirself. _____

6 The young couple didn't plan to have no children. _____

7 We should have submitted them forms by the first of the month. _____

8 Jeremy grew up as a heir to a rubber tire fortune. _____

9 We ourself never left any garbage at the campsites. _____

10 The suspect was a unemployed accountant. _____

11 Them young people in the truck had nowhere to stay. _____

12 The new neighbors made it clear they didn't want no advice. _____

13 During an hour's drive, we never saw no stop sign or traffic light. _____

14 The package that is now two dollar used to be 80 cents. _____

15 They never could have solved the problem by theirself. _____

CAPSULE RULE Decide whether to use a comma or a semicolon when linking two complete statements.

1 Use a **semicolon** between two paired statements with *no* connecting word like *and* or *therefore*. You are just putting two closely related statements next to each other:

SEMICOLON: Carol lives at home; she just moved back.

2 Use a **comma** before a coordinator (coordinating conjunction). There are seven of these: *and, but, for, so, or, nor, yet.*

COMMA: The lights dimmed, **and** the crowd roared.
Stock prices soared, **but** teachers' salaries stayed low.
We discontinued the program, **for** the funds ran out.
The supply dried up, **so** prices rose.

3 Use a **semicolon** when a connecting adverb like *however* or *therefore* links two statements. Put the semicolon at the break between the two statements, regardless of where the connecting word appears in the second statement. Other words like *however* include *nevertheless, furthermore, moreover, accordingly, besides, indeed,* and *in fact.* (These words are also called *conjunctive adverbs* or *adverbial conjunctions.* In formal writing, commas set these words off from the second statement.)

SEMICOLON: Attendance was poor; **therefore,** we canceled the show.
Attendance was poor; we canceled the show, **therefore.**
Attendance was poor; management, **therefore,** canceled the show.

BACKUP EXPLANATION

When we **coordinate** two statements, we combine two statements that are equally important. They could easily be separated again by a period. The handiest link is a coordinator: *and, but, for, so, or, nor, yet.* Use a comma before these—but only when they actually join two statements—each with a subject and a verb: Unions (S) ask (V) us to buy American, **but** the customers (S) buy (V) Japanese. Connecting adverbs—*however, therefore, nevertheless, indeed*— are movable adverbs—like other adverbs. The semicolon stays where the two statements are joined:

The weather turned ugly; **therefore,** the launch was postponed.
The trial date was set; the defendant, **however,** had disappeared.
Mozart struggled financially; he died poor, **in fact.**

PROBLEM SPOTTER

Can you see the problem in each of the following examples and how the problem was corrected?

NO: A pawnshop is downstairs, above it is a hotel.
YES: **A pawnshop is downstairs; above it is a hotel.**
NO: The college accepted me but, housing was a problem.
YES: **The college accepted me, but housing was a problem.**

NO:	The thin look was in, therefore yogurt sales soared.
YES:	**The thin look was in; therefore, yogurt sales soared.**
NO:	Terrorists were hijacking planes we booked our trip nevertheless.
YES:	**Terrorists were hijacking planes; we booked our trip, nevertheless.**
NO:	The teacher disliked the children and the parents knew it.
YES:	**The teacher disliked the children, and the parents knew it.**

INSTANT REVIEW

Check punctuation—which sentences are right? Which are wrong? Mark each sentence S for satisfactory or U for unsatisfactory.

1 The weather turned ugly, therefore the launch was postponed.   ____

2 The police moved in, and the protesters fell back.   ____

3 Salmon used to go upstream; now, however, the river is dammed.   ____

4 We need to lighten the load, or the boat will swamp.   ____

5 People bootleg new miracle drugs, for the approval process is slow.   ____

6 They had been warned; they crashed the party, nevertheless.   ____

7 The concert was canceled the star was sick.   ____

8 Few Anglos worked there, the manager was Chinese in fact.   ____

9 The pilots were on strike; all flights were canceled.   ____

10 The *Titanic* radioed for help but, no one heard.   ____

FINER POINTS

■ Words like *and, but, or,* and *for* do not always join two complete statements, each with its own subject and verb. Do *not* use a comma when these words join two parts of a single statement:

NO COMMA: The government banned Western music **and many books.**
He was always collecting specimens **or looking for arrowheads in the woods.**
They had saved some tickets **for regular customers.**

■ The extra commas with words like *therefore* and *however* are often left out in modern prose, especially in informal and journalistic writing:

SEMICOLON ONLY: The snow had stopped; the roads **however** were still closed.

Name _____

EDITING PRACTICE

Punctuate the following combined sentences. In each blank space, enter a comma or a semicolon. Or leave the space blank if there should be no punctuation.

1   Jobs were scarce _____ so my parents left town.

2   Space exploration costs millions _____ therefore, only rich nations take part.

3   She was not a big-time photographer _____ but she made enough to survive.

4   Meteors bombarded the surface _____ they left huge craters.

5   The Russians led in the space race _____ their cosmonauts set endurance records.

6   The Russians launched the first satellite _____ but the Americans were first on the moon.

7   She was not a citizen _____ her application therefore was turned down.

8   Terrorists attacked airports and cruise ships _____ and the tourists stayed away.

9   Jacques tried to reform _____ his father disinherited him, nevertheless.

10   We need to protect the gorillas _____ for they may soon be extinct.

11   Wages stagnated _____ executive salaries zoomed.

12   You should not call her there _____ besides, the line is always busy.

13   The car was expensive _____ but the rebate made it a good buy.

14   The party touts free enterprise _____ therefore, it favors deregulation.

15   Henry and I are alike _____ we both love science fiction.

16   Their support did not help _____ it was a liability, in fact.

17   The meeting received no publicity _____ the turnout, accordingly, was small.

18   We should apologize _____ or we will never be asked again.

19   The picnic fizzled _____ for it started to rain.

20   He wanted to marry her _____ her parents, however, said no.

SENTENCE PRACTICE—YOUR TURN

A Write five sentences that pair two complete statements, linking them with *and, but, so, for, or, nor,* or *yet.* Use the comma.

EXAMPLE: Baseball is the great American pastime, **but** soccer is the great national pastime in Europe.

_____

_____

_____

_____

_____

_____

_____

_____

_____

_____

B Write five sentences that pair two complete statements. Link them with a word like *however, therefore, nevertheless, furthermore, besides, indeed,* or *in fact.* Use the semicolon.

EXAMPLE: So-called experts predicted low attendance for the Women's World Cup; **however,** record crowds proved them wrong.

_____

_____

_____

_____

_____

_____

_____

_____

_____

_____

CAPSULE RULE Use no comma when you bring essential conditions or specifications into a sentence.

1   **Subordinators** (subordinating conjunctions) like *if, unless, while, when, before,* or *until* usually bring essential conditions into a sentence: a rebate **if you act now** (only if you act now); no dessert **until you finish your beans** (not until then). The added statement narrows or restricts the meaning of the sentence. It is **restrictive**—NO COMMA.

2   Some subordinators—*though, although, whereas, no matter how*—are different. They leave the main point of the sentence unchanged. The main point of the sentence is true regardless. These subordinators merely bring in something that is also true. The added material is **nonrestrictive**—USE A COMMA.

   COMMA: Attendance was poor, **although** we had a good team.
   COMMA: Sharks are fish, **whereas** whales are mammals.
   COMMA: The concerts were sold out, **no matter how** early we got in line.

3   If the subordinator starts the sentence (as in this example), use the comma regardless—no matter whether the added point is essential or not.

   COMMA: **If you act now,** you will get a rebate.
   COMMA: **Unless you finish your beans,** there will be no dessert.

BACKUP EXPLANATION

■   Subordinators bring in an additional **clause**—a second group of words that also has its own subject and complete verb:

   MAIN CLAUSE: **Marcia** (S) **was** (V) a junior.
   ADDED CLAUSE: Marcia was a junior when **the rules** (S) **were changed** (V).

■   The added second clause cannot simply be unhooked again. It becomes a **dependent** clause. It has to stay with the main clause. If you set it off by a period, you get a **sentence fragment:**

   FRAGMENT: Inflation slows down. *When oil prices fall.*
   CORRECTED: Inflation slows down **when oil prices fall.**
   FRAGMENT: The left brain is analytical. *Whereas the right brain is intuitive.*
   CORRECTED: The left brain is analytical, **whereas the right brain is intuitive.**

PROBLEM SPOTTER

   Can you see the problem in each of the following examples? Can you see how the problem was corrected?

   NO: Coastal cities will be submerged. If the ice cap melts.
   YES: **Coastal cities will be submerged if the ice cap melts.**
   NO: Evolution is gradual. Whereas revolution is sudden.
   YES: **Evolution is gradual, whereas revolution is sudden.**
   NO: If you don't register you can't vote.
   YES: **If you don't register, you can't vote.**

NO: We will all perish. Unless rescuers arrive.
YES: **We will all perish unless rescuers arrive.**
NO: He was touched, when we sent him the singing telegram.
YES: **He was touched when we sent him the singing telegram.**

INSTANT REVIEW

Which of the following examples have the right punctuation? Write Yes or No.

1 Salmon gather in large groups before they go up the river. _____

2 Nuclear energy will be phased out. Unless nuclear wastes can be safely stored. _____

3 When spring returned Easter rituals took place. _____

4 The Greeks built theaters, whereas the Romans built arenas. _____

5 We felt the aftershocks. Although we were fifty miles away. _____

6 Children love stories where the ugly duckling turns into a swan. _____

7 If you don't vote, you should not complain. _____

8 East Germans hated the wall, no matter what their government said. _____

9 The valley will be flooded, unless we reinforce the dams. _____

10 They kept a candle in the window. Until the prisoners returned. _____

FINER POINTS

1 Use a **comma** with *because* if the main point comes before the *because*. Use no comma if the main point comes after the *because*.

   WHAT DECISION? **We are definitely moving,** because I cannot find a job.
   WHAT REASON? We are moving **only because I cannot find a job.**

2 Use a **semicolon** between the two clauses if a *though* comes later in the second clause:

   SEMICOLON: The potatoes were burnt; **the fish, though, was delicious.**
   (used like *nevertheless*)

3 Use a comma with *however* if it means "no matter how":

   They snubbed us, **however** (no matter how) **hard we tried.**

Name _____

REVISION PRACTICE

Punctuate the following combined sentences. Enter a comma when it is needed. Or leave the space blank if there should be no punctuation. Some of the following examples add two dependent clauses to the original sentence.

1 You cannot get the refund _____ unless you have your receipt.

2 If the witnesses do not testify _____ they will be in contempt of court.

3 If you leave your number _____ we will call you _____ when the merchandise arrives.

4 He befriended the unfortunate _____ although he was poor himself.

5 Jesters tell bitter truths _____ whereas clowns just clown around.

6 The team will leave _____ if the voters vote against a new stadium.

7 While the orchestra played _____ spectators were munching popcorn.

8 Spiked hair became fashionable _____ when punk rock hit the charts.

9 They decided to wait _____ until the rain stopped _____ although they were already late.

10 The car will be towed _____ no matter how much the motorist complains.

11 The phone will be disconnected _____ unless the customer pays.

12 If you speak two languages _____ you are bilingual.

13 Bystanders pulled the motorist out _____ before the car burst into flames.

14 The accused enjoys legal safeguards _____ whereas the victim is forgotten.

15 Surfers may have to wait for hours _____ until the waves are right.

16 Although the commute was bad _____ Lydia rarely missed class.

17 Child care remained a problem _____ no matter how hard parents tried.

18 Professional writers may do several rewrites _____ before they are satisfied.

19 Tax forms became more complicated _____ although Congress had promised simpler laws.

20 Before the new CEO was appointed _____ few women had been top managers of Fortune 500 companies.

SENTENCE PRACTICE—YOUR TURN

A Write five sentences that pair two complete statements each, linking them with a subordinator like *if, unless, when, before, after,* or *until*—NO COMMA.

EXAMPLE: We will cancel the game if it rains. (we'll do it only then)

_____

_____

_____

_____

_____

_____

_____

_____

_____

_____

B Write five sentences that pair two complete statements each, linking them with a subordinator like *although, whereas, no matter how,* or *no matter what*—USE THE COMMA.

EXAMPLE: Climbers scale treacherous mountains, although each year climbers get killed. (they do it *regardless*)

_____

_____

_____

_____

_____

_____

_____

_____

_____

_____

_____

CAPSULE RULE   Use no comma when a word like *who* or *that* brings in material that narrows our choices.

1   Use *no comma* when a **relative pronoun**—*who (whom, whose), which,* or *that*—brings in material that narrows down or restricts what the original sentence said. The added material then is **restrictive.** It is needed to tell us which one or what kind—NO COMMA:

WHICH ONE?   The convict **who escaped** was serving a life sentence.
WHAT KIND?   She loved people **who had a sense of humor.**
WHICH ONE?   The town **that they remembered** no longer existed.

2   Use *a comma* when the relative pronoun follows something that is already known or identified. The added material then is **nonrestrictive.** It is not needed to pinpoint something or to single it out.

OPTIONAL INFO: They lived in Baltimore, **which has marvelous seafood.**
OPTIONAL INFO: He blamed Congress, **which had stalled the legislation.**

3   Use *two commas* when nonrestrictive material interrupts the sentence:

TWO COMMAS: Buffaloes, **which used to roam the plains,** were almost extinct.
                          Bill Gates, **who developed Windows,** became a billionaire.

BACKUP EXPLANATION

The relative pronouns are *who* (also *whom* and *whose), which,* and *that.* They join a relative clause to a noun or pronoun in the original sentence. (We link them to *a specific part* of the original sentence.) They bring into the sentence material like the following: motorists **who speed;** computers **that crash;** President Nixon, **who resigned in disgrace;** condors, **which were once almost extinct;** drivers **whose licenses have been suspended.** In most of these examples, the relative pronoun serves as the subject of the added clause:

RELATIVE CLAUSE: Birds at first may have been dinosaurs **that (S) learned (V) to fly.**

■   The added relative clause cannot simply be unhooked again. It becomes a **dependent** clause and has to stay with the **main clause.** If you set it off by a period, you get a sentence fragment:

FRAGMENT: They were fans of Madonna. *Who played Evita.*
CORRECTED: They were fans of Madonna, **who played Evita.**
FRAGMENT: They sold T-shirts. *Which carried colorful messages.*
CORRECTED: They sold T-shirts, **which carried colorful messages.**

PROBLEM SPOTTER

Can you see the problem in each of the following examples? Can you see how the problem was corrected?

NO: The board fired the president. Who had founded the company.
YES: **The board fired the president, who had founded the company.**

NO:	The inquiry centered on players, who received recruitment bonuses.
YES:	**The inquiry centered on players who received recruitment bonuses.**
NO:	Buildings that were condemned, had to be torn down.
YES:	**Buildings that were condemned had to be torn down.**
NO:	Karl Marx who wrote *Das Kapital* lived in England.
YES:	**Karl Marx, who wrote *Das Kapital*, lived in England.**
NO:	Two brothers had the winning number. Which was good for two million dollars.
YES:	**Two brothers had the winning number, which was good for two million dollars.**

INSTANT REVIEW

Which of the following examples have the right punctuation? Write Yes or No.

1   Riders who don't wear helmets take foolish risks.   _____

2   President Clinton who hobnobbed with world leaders had been a poor boy in Arkansas.   _____

3   Their checks were like Confederate money, which is worthless.   _____

4   She admired her mother, who was a pacifist.   _____

5   Ralph Nader who attacked giant corporations became famous as a consumer advocate.   _____

6   The evil that men do lives after them. (Shakespeare)   _____

7   Highbrow critics hate movies that have happy endings.   _____

8   Washington, which is our capital, might also be the murder capital of the nation.   _____

9   Japanese cars which required few repairs became popular.   _____

10   The book told the story of Madame Curie, who was a French scientist.   _____

FINER POINTS

1   A relative clause starting with *that* is always restrictive:

NO COMMA:	He left after the revolution **that swept Iran.**
NO COMMA:	The drought **that lasted three months** finally ended.

A relative clause with a *that* or *whom* left out is always restrictive:

NO COMMA:	The convertible (that) **she bought** made her friends envious.
NO COMMA:	The speaker (whom) **he signed up** canceled her appearance.

2   Many dependent clauses starting with **that** are *not* relative clauses. They take the place of a noun after verbs like *say, announce, ask,* or *deny.* We call them **noun clauses.** Many dependent clauses starting with *why, what,* or *how* work the same way. NO COMMA WITH NOUN CLAUSES:

NO COMMA:	The memo said **that employees could not receive private e-mail.**
NO COMMA:	Every wondered **how the policy would be enforced.**

3   Use *who* to point back to people. Use *which* to point back to animals and things.

WHO:	The company hired a guard, **who** patrolled the grounds.
WHICH:	The neighbors bought a dog, **which** barked all night.

Name _____

Punctuate the following combined sentences. Enter commas where they are needed. Or leave the space blank if there should be no punctuation. Some of the following examples add two relative clauses to the original sentence.

1   Space probes _____ that photographed Jupiter _____ sent back amazing pictures.

2   Contestants _____ who lost _____ congratulated those _____ who won.

3   Penicillin _____ which saved many lives _____ was discovered by accident.

4   Couples _____ who married young _____ had a high divorce rate.

5   We bypassed Yellowstone Park _____ which was in flames.

6   The court banned tests _____ that discriminated against minorities.

7   The driver _____ whose car blocked the driveway _____ is in big trouble.

8   Egg yolks _____ which are high in cholesterol _____ disappeared from many recipes.

9   He was the kind of candidate _____ who campaigns year-round.

10 The pictures _____ that we saw _____ showed people _____ who had lost everything.

11 Drivers _____ who lose their licenses _____ often drive without them.

12 Vietnam _____ which had been a French colony _____ became a Communist nation.

13 The tour group went to Jamaica _____ which used to be British.

14 Citizens _____ who have complaints _____ should be able to voice them.

15 Firms _____ that tow illegally parked cars _____ are hated by everyone.

16 The groom _____ who looked very serious _____ had already been married four times.

17 Students _____ who need assistance _____ can apply for loans _____ that carry low interest rates.

18 Shirley met with her best friend _____ whose book had just received an award.

19 Lenin's tomb _____ which is visited by millions of tourists _____ was closed for repairs.

20 Manuel _____ who was an experienced actor _____ still suffered from stage fright.

SENTENCE PRACTICE—YOUR TURN

A   Write five sentences that pair two complete statements each, linking them with a relative pronoun like *who, whose, whom,* or *that.* Use the relative pronoun to bring in essential (restrictive) information—NO COMMA.

EXAMPLE: Pilots who fly small planes are not always well trained.

_____

_____

_____

_____

_____

_____

_____

_____

_____

_____

B   Write five sentences that pair two complete statements each, linking them with a relative pronoun like *who, whose, whom,* or *which.* Use the relative pronoun to bring in optional added (nonrestrictive) information—USE COMMAS AS NEEDED.

EXAMPLE: We decided to rent a scanner, which feeds printed text into a computer.

_____

_____

_____

_____

_____

_____

_____

_____

_____

_____

CAPSULE RULE Use no comma when modifiers add essential information to a sentence.

1 **Restrictive** modifiers give essential information about how, when, where, or why. Or they specify which one or what kind. Such modifiers are needed to narrow things down—they are restrictive: NO COMMA.

WHICH ONE? The pedestrian **hit by the car** sued the motorist.
WHAT KIND? Reporters **spying on celebrities** are called *paparazzi.*
WHICH ONE? The teacher **from the inner city** received an award for excellence.

2 **Nonrestrictive** modifiers add optional information about something already nailed down or identified. Set them off by COMMAS. Use two commas if needed—before and after the added detail:

ADDED DETAIL: The voters chose Bill Clinton, **a former governor of Arkansas.**
ADDED DETAIL: Mick Jagger, **dancing around the stage,** made the crowd roar.

3 When a modifier comes first, set it off to show where the main part of the sentence starts. Use the comma after the **introductory modifier** regardless of whether it's nonrestrictive.

COMMA: **When hunting,** lions avoid wooded areas.
COMMA: **When hunting lions,** avoid wooded areas.

BACKUP EXPLANATION

■ **Prepositional phrases** are groups of words starting with a preposition like *at, by, on, to, with, without, over,* or *above.* They are usually restrictive. They come into a sentence without a break: parked **at** the station; a suspect **on** the run; left **without** permission. However, if the prepositional phrase comes first, use a comma if the phrase has three words or more:

NO COMMA: Solar energy has real potential **in a sunny climate.**
COMMA: **In a sunny climate,** solar energy has real potential.

■ An **appositive** is a second noun that comes into a sentence as an added label: Johnny Cochran, **the lawyer;** Gilroy, **the garlic capital** of the West. The appositive usually adds optional information (we can pinpoint the person or the place without it). Use a COMMA, or TWO COMMAS if needed.

COMMA: The statue was of Cortez, **the Spanish conquistador.**
COMMAS: Her brother, **a diabetic,** took insulin.

■ **Verbals** are words that look like verbs but are not used as complete verbs in a sentence. Many of them are *-ing* forms like *knowing, resting, having answered,* or *being sought.* Many are *to* forms (infinitives) like *to know, to investigate,* or *to be completed.* Many verbals are forms that would normally follow a world like *have:* (have) *known,* (have) *taken,* (have) *accepted,* (have) *rejected.*

141

Verbals can go either way. They may be used restrictively to narrow things down—NO COMMA: the manual **accompanying the computer**; the enemy soldiers **taken prisoner**. Or they may be used to add nonessential detail—COMMA, or TWO COMMAS if needed: Apple, **struggling to stay competitive**; IBM, **dominating the market**.

WHICH ONE? (NO COMMA): The guard **watching the hostages** was asleep.
ADDED DETAIL (COMMAS): His bodyguard, **riding next to him**, was killed.

Set off all **introductory verbals** regardless of whether the material they bring in is essential or not:

COMMA: **Trailing by ten points**, her team never gave up.

PROBLEM SPOTTER

Can you see the problem in each of the following examples? Can you see how the problem was corrected?

NO: The new computers had no slots for floppies considered obsolete.
YES: **The new computers had no slots for floppies, considered obsolete.**
NO: After the near meltdown the reactor was enclosed in cement.
YES: **After the near meltdown, the reactor was enclosed in cement.**
NO: Hikers entering the park, are warned against snakes.
YES: **Hikers entering the park are warned against snakes.**
NO: Ronald Reagan the great communicator charmed voters with his smile.
YES: **Ronald Reagan, the great communicator, charmed voters with his smile.**
NO: Our candidate trailing badly, conceded defeat.
YES: **Our candidate, trailing badly, conceded defeat.**

INSTANT REVIEW

Put a check mark next to each sentence that has the right punctuation.

1 Whitman, the American poet, celebrated the new continent.   _____

2 Women walking alone took grave risks.   _____

3 The officer writing the ticket, looked familiar.   _____

4 Trees, dropping their leaves, are deciduous.   _____

5 Without the least warning the officers fired their guns.   _____

6 Wanted by the police in five states, Herman finally surrendered.   _____

7 They took us to their favorite place, a Chinese restaurant.   _____

8 Chairman Mao creator of the New China had just died.   _____

9 At great personal risk, they sheltered the refugees.   _____

10 Fans still mourn Elvis Presley, the king of Rock 'n Roll.   _____

FINER POINTS

An appositive is a second noun that provides a label for the first: my mother-in-law, **the doctor**; McDonald's, **symbol of American civilization**. Appositives are usually nonrestrictive—they tell us more about something already pinned down. But sometimes we use an appositive to tell two things apart—NO COMMA:

NO COMMA: I don't mean Jean Flanagan **the doctor**; I mean Jean Flanagan **the coach**.

Name _____

Punctuate the following sentences. Enter commas where they are needed. Or leave the space blank if there should be no punctuation. You may have to check punctuation for more than one modifier brought into the same sentence.

1   The platform appealed strongly to Canadians _____ speaking French.

2   Caught in the middle _____ the coach tried to make peace.

3   Columbus _____ an Italian navigator _____ was looking for India.

4   Researchers _____ looking for the AIDS virus _____ were successful.

5   The company sold parts _____ for British motorcycles.

6   Computers _____ developed in America _____ are now mostly made overseas.

7   Working feverishly _____ the rescuers freed the motorist _____ trapped in the car.

8   The speaker was Sandra O'Connor _____ the Supreme Court Justice.

9   To retrieve voice-mail _____ users needed a special access code.

10   According to the plaintiffs _____ the money should go to those _____ hurt by the scam.

11   Plagued by huge deficits _____ high-speed trains connect major European cities.

12   Bears _____ protecting their cubs _____ are fierce fighters.

13   We visited Gettysburg _____ the site of a famous battle.

14   The Vietnam War Memorial _____ visited by thousands _____ commemorates our dead.

15   The poem was about Buffalo Bill _____ a famous killer.

16   The poster attacked hunters _____ clubbing baby seals.

17   Burning out of control _____ the fire lit up the sky.

18   For the first time _____ management listened _____ to workers' grievances.

19   Archeologists rarely find a tomb _____ not plundered by robbers.

20   *Star Trek* _____ canceled by the network _____ lived on in reruns.

SENTENCE PRACTICE—YOUR TURN

A Write five sentences that use an appositive to bring in nonessential added detail. Use COMMAS as needed.

EXAMPLE: A runaway boy and an escaped slave, an odd couple for their time, travel down the Mississippi.

_____

_____

_____

_____

_____

_____

_____

_____

_____

_____

B Write five sentences that use verbals to bring information into a sentence. Use COMMAS as needed.

EXAMPLE: Dinosaurs, combining large bodies and small heads, became extinct.

_____

_____

_____

_____

_____

_____

_____

_____

_____

_____

CAPSULE RULE   Use commas with several sentence parts of the same kind.

1   Use commas between parts of a **series**—three or more sentence parts of the same kind: **male, single,** and **twenty-one; fruit, vegetables,** and **flowers; administrators, teachers,** and **students.**

> COMMAS: **Brazil, Italy, and France** were the superpowers of soccer.
> COMMAS: The vase **swayed, toppled over, and crashed on the floor.**

2   Use commas with information that comes in several parts, such as addresses (**192 First Street, Morristown, Montana**) and measurements (**six foot, three inches**). Especially, use the comma between city and state:

> COMMAS: We moved from **Baltimore, Maryland,** to **Los Angeles, California.**

3   Use commas between **interchangeable adjectives**: a **fast-moving, exciting** game (same as an exciting, fast-moving game); **juicy, tasty** fruit (same as tasty, juicy fruit). Not all adjectives are interchangeable (no comma): a **brilliant nuclear** physicist (but not a nuclear brilliant physicist).

BACKUP EXPLANATION

- A series may be a set of three *or more*. Often a series follows a **colon** to fill in details for something already summarized:

> COMMAS: The square was bustling with **tourists, vendors, police, and pickpockets.**
> (four items in a series)
> COLON: They loved tropical fruit: **oranges, pineapple, and bananas.**

- If the sentence *continues*, use an additional comma at the end of an address—but not measurements:

> ADDRESSES: The family moved from **Fish Avenue, Bensenhurst, New Jersey,** to **Park Avenue, New York, New York.**
> MEASURES: **Six foot, four inches** was no longer unusual for a player.

- With true interchangeable adjectives, an *and* may take the place of the comma: **torn, dirty jeans** (same as torn and dirty jeans); a **tall, handsome** stranger (same as a tall and handsome stranger).

PROBLEM SPOTTER

NO: The candidate had never been engaged married or divorced.
YES: **The candidate had never been engaged, married, or divorced.**
NO: They moved from Lubbock Texas to Albuquerque New Mexico.
YES: **They moved from Lubbock, Texas, to Albuquerque, New Mexico.**
NO: She spoke three languages English French and Vietnamese.
YES: **She spoke three languages: English, French, and Vietnamese.**
NO: Sean had been a responsible reliable worker.
YES: **Sean had been a responsible, reliable worker.**
NO: Average height was six foot three inches.
YES: **Average height was six foot, three inches.**

INSTANT REVIEW

Which of the following examples have the right punctuation? Write Yes or No.

1   The head office was in Hartford Connecticut.   _____

2   We have changed from an active, low-calorie way of life to a passive, high-calorie lifestyle.   _____

3   The center staff studies robotics, artificial intelligence, and waste management.   _____

4   Highly paid public servants received generous pensions.   _____

5   The Mayans built temples palaces and pyramids.   _____

6   The new manager was petty, inexperienced, and vindictive.   _____

7   The menu featured tortillas, and refried beans.   _____

8   Drunk drivers weave from lane to lane cross dividers and go up ramps the wrong way.   _____

9   Some species prosper in the desert: lizards, cactus, and mesquite.   _____

10 Six foot four inches was the average height of the players.   _____

FINER POINTS

Here are some additional comma rules:

1   Use commas to highlight a *contrast:*

    Workers were laid off at **the American plants, not the plants overseas.**

2   Use commas to signal *repetition:*

    They always wanted **the finest, the best.**

3   Use commas to set off *tags and tag questions:*

    Well, they did their best, **didn't they?**
    Why, we hardly knew him.

4   Use commas to set off *comments and other interrupters:*

    His license, **it seems,** had expired.
    These dreams, **my friends,** will not come true.

Name _____

Punctuate the following sentences. Enter commas or other punctuation where needed. Or leave the space blank if there should be no punctuation.

1   The residents _____ were tired of gangs _____ drugs _____ and violence.

2   New cars use plastics for many parts _____ fenders _____ bumpers _____ and control panels.

3   The Beatles came from Liverpool _____ England.

4   The irritable _____ short-tempered _____ advisor talked to the new _____ chemistry majors.

5   The band played in Phoenix _____ Arizona _____ Houston _____ Texas _____ and

    Las Vegas _____ Nevada.

6   Jeans _____ T-shirts _____ and hamburgers _____ became popular in Europe.

7   The trend is toward natural _____ organic foods.

8   The car _____ went out of control _____ spun around _____ and crashed into the divider.

9   There were many _____ Spanish-speaking immigrants _____ Mexicans _____ Puerto Ricans _____ and Cubans.

10 Chanting _____ flag-waving _____ demonstrators jammed the square.

11 Her family liked hearty food _____ meat _____ potatoes _____ and gravy.

12 Alligators _____ mosquitoes _____ and malaria kept settlers _____ away from the swamps.

13 Chicago _____ Illinois _____ and Los Angeles _____ California _____ are among _____ our biggest cities.

14 The company had moved _____ to 34 Bird Street _____ Heronsville _____ Louisiana.

15 The Boeing Company built furniture _____ sea planes _____ and finally modern airliners.

16 Her old-fashioned _____ conservative parents frowned on loud _____ garish clothes.

17 The numbers of the homeless _____ the unemployed _____ and the underemployed _____ were growing.

18 The panel focused on date rape _____ marital rape _____ and sexual abuse.

19 Their blond _____ blue-eyed Swedish friend measured six foot _____ two inches.

20 The eruption of the volcano _____ destroyed acres of forests _____ caused millions in

    property damage _____ and killed 57 people.

SENTENCE PRACTICE—YOUR TURN

A Write five sentences with three or more items of the same kind in a series.

EXAMPLES: Resentment, confusion, and frustration are often the result of forced retirement.

People protest against abortion by various means: picketing, speeches, demonstrations, arson, and murder.

_____

_____

_____

_____

_____

_____

B Write three sentences giving the full addresses of real or imaginary firms and persons.

_____

_____

_____

_____

_____

_____

_____

C Write five sentences packed with adjectives, using commas where required.

EXAMPLE: An eccentric elderly gentleman revives the DNA of long dead dinosaurs and bloodthirsty, merciless marauders.

_____

_____

_____

_____

_____

_____

_____

PUNCTUATING QUOTATIONS

CAPSULE RULE   Use quotation marks when you repeat someone's exact words.

Use **quotation marks** to signal the beginning and the end of a quotation. Copy the material you enclose in quotation marks exactly word for word.

1   Put a **comma** after the introductory source statement or **credit tag**. Put the comma *before* the opening quotation mark. Use a comma also if the credit tag comes at the end. Put the comma before the closing quotation mark (inside the quotation).

COMMA: The doctor said, **"The test results are negative."**
       "The deadline has passed," the letter said.

Use a **colon** after the credit tag to give the quotation extra emphasis:

COLON: The article made the point very strongly: **"Excessive tanning is bad for your health."**

2   Use **two commas** when the credit tag splits *one* complete statement. However, use a comma before and a period (or semicolon) after if the credit tag splits *two* complete statements:

SPLIT: **"Applications received after June 1,"** the announcement read, **"cannot be considered."**
SPLIT: **"Computers are becoming more powerful,"** the ad said. **"At the same time, they are becoming cheaper."**

3   Use **no comma** or colon if a few quoted words become part of your sentence.

NO COMMA: The candidate claimed to be a **"compassionate conservative."**
         The mayor called the neighborhood a **"war zone."**

BACKUP EXPLANATION

Use quotation marks for **direct quotation.** You are using direct quotation when you quote someone verbatim, exactly word for word. However, use *no* quotation marks for **indirect quotation**—when you report what someone else said or wrote but you put it in your own words.

DIRECT: The tour director said: **"I expect** everyone at the bus at eight o'clock."
INDIRECT: The tour director said **she expected** everyone at the bus at eight o'clock.
       (The director refers to herself as *I*, but you refer to her as *she*. She was talking about the present, but you report it as something that happened in the past. NO QUOTATION MARKS.)
DIRECT: The lecturer told the audience: **"You can judge** a civilization by how it treats prisoners, the destitute, and the mentally ill."
INDIRECT: The lecturer told the audience **that they could** judge a civilization by how it **treated** prisoners, the destitute, and the mentally ill.

PROBLEM SPOTTER

Can you see the problem in each of the following examples? Can you see how the problem was corrected?

NO: The sign said: Better active today than radioactive tomorrow.
YES: **The sign said: "Better active today than radioactive tomorrow."**

NO:	The letter began, the better mousetrap has been built.
YES:	**The letter began, "The better mousetrap has been built."**
NO:	"This day, the speaker said, marks the beginning of an era."
YES:	**"This day," the speaker said, "marks the beginning of an era."**
NO:	"This is not the beginning of the end," Churchill said, "it is the end of the beginning."
YES:	**"This is not the beginning of the end," Churchill said. "It is the end of the beginning."**
NO:	The mayor announced "that she would not run for reelection."
YES:	**The mayor announced that she would not run for reelection.**

FINER POINTS

1   Check **end punctuation** with your quotations. A comma or a period at the end comes *before* the closing quotation mark. A semicolon comes *after*.

COMMA:	"Every student will be computer-literate," the governor said.
PERIOD:	The author claimed: "Hand-held computers are around the corner."
SEMICOLON:	The superintendent said, "Talk is cheap"; the funding was just not available.

When you quote a **question** or a **strong remark**, the question mark or the exclamation mark belongs with the quotation. It comes *before* the closing quotation mark. However sometimes you ask a question, or you make a strong point, *about* a quotation. The question mark or exclamation mark then is *not* part of the quotation. It goes outside the closing quotation mark.

QUOTED QUESTION:	The ad asked: "Are you paying too much for phone service?"
QUESTIONED QUOTE:	Did the ad say: "Six months of long distance free"?
QUOTED WARNING:	*Consumer Reports* warned: "The interest rate triples after three months!"
WARNING QUOTE:	The fine print read: "All decisions are final"!

2   Show any changes you have made in your quoted material. Maybe you left out part of a very long quotation—to make the main point stand out. Use *three spaced periods* (an **ellipsis**) to show the *omission* or deletion. (Use four if you cut something after a sentence period.)

OMISSION:	According to the U.N. report, "The AIDS epidemic . . . is ravaging large parts of Africa."

Sometimes you will insert a needed *explanation* or correction into a quotation. Put the added material in **square brackets**:

ADDITION:	According to the author, "The British influence was still strong in Nigeria and Zimbabwe [the former Rhodesia]."

Name _____

REVISION PRACTICE

Punctuate the following sentences. Enter quotation marks and other punctuation where they are needed. Or leave the space blank if there should be no punctuation.

1   "It was a sudden inspiration _____ the researcher said.

2   She said, "A six-month jump on a competitor is worth money _____

3   "The new coating," they explained _____ forms a kind of thermal brake _____

4   The ad offered "Cable TV Secrets that cable companies tried to ban _____

5   The announcement was greeted with shouts of "Resign! Resign _____

6   "We are truly sorry," the letter said _____ We have to return your application _____

7   Is it true that he repeatedly said: "Your investment is safe _____

8   The headline shouted: "Survivor Found After Three Weeks _____

9   The article claimed _____ that colonization of Mars was possible _____

10 "New ceramics and plastics," the article said _____ will replace steel and copper _____

11 "Off-road vehicles _____ the expert said _____ are rough on the environment _____

12 The secretary replied _____ No comment _____ to most of the questions.

13 The principal said _____ that he would not tolerate inappropriate behavior _____

14 "Today is the 4th _____ the note read _____ Where is the rent _____

15 According to the author, the women's movement had entered "the second phase _____

16 "Now is the time _____ the speaker said _____ to take a stand."

17 She asked, "When will peace finally come to this war-torn country _____

18 The tourist asked _____ whether the painting was an original _____

19 "Changes are inevitable _____ the speaker said _____

20 The final sentence read _____ Species that are endangered today will be extinct tomorrow _____

SENTENCE PRACTICE: WORDS OF THE WEEK

As you read newspapers or magazines, do you notice sayings that stand out? Look for statements that strike you as particularly educational, thought-provoking, funny, or ignorant. Select between five and ten as "Words of the Week." Write them down as **quotable quotes** accompanied by a short introductory statement or credit tag. Prepare to share your choices with your classmates.

EXAMPLE: The editorial said, "Young voters are staying away from the polls."

_____

_____

_____

_____

_____

_____

_____

_____

_____

_____

_____

_____

_____

_____

_____

_____

_____

_____

_____

_____

_____

_____

_____

_____

CAPSULE RULE Use the apostrophe for the possessive—to show where something belongs.

Possessives are special forms showing that one thing belongs or relates to another: (the dirt bike owned by her cousin) her **cousin's dirt bike;** (the farm that belonged to the family) the **family's farm;** (the mansion lived in by the governor) the **governor's mansion;** (the concert scheduled today) **today's concert.**

1 For most **singular nouns**, add *both* the apostrophe and the *-s* ending: (one) the **boy's** smile, (one) the oldest **sister's** graduation, (one) the **officer's** motorcycle. Read the examples over several times:

   APOSTROPHE + s: the **lawyer's** fee, her **dentist's** office, the **traveler's** reservation, my **driver's** license, the **trainer's** schedule

2 Most **plural nouns** already have a final *-s* to show more than one: both *sisters*, several *officers*, too many *lawyers*. To change these plural nouns to the possessive, add the **apostrophe only:** his **sister's** degree (one sister)—his **sisters'** degrees (several sisters). Watch changes in spelling: one **family's** savings—both **families'** savings; one **country's** government—both **countries'** governments.

   APOSTROPHE ONLY: several **lawyers'** fees, both **brothers'** birthdays, low **waitresses'** wages, both **coworkers'** laptops

3 Plurals without a plural *-s* (*men, women, children*) use the normal possessive form—*both* apostrophe and added ending:

   APOSTROPHE + s: **men's** clothing, **women's** rights, **children's** toys, **people's** manners

4 Many **pronouns** have a normal possessive form: to **everyone's** surprise, **nobody's** business, at **one's** own risk, **someone else's** responsibility. However, the **possessive** pronouns **hers, its** (when used to show belonging), **ours, yours,** and **theirs** are important exceptions—**no** apostrophe: He paid for his purchases and she for **hers.**

   NO APOSTROPHE: We could not agree whether the tickets were **ours** or **theirs.**

5 Use the apostrophe with many expressions pinpointing time or value: **today's** news, **yesterday's** events, **tomorrow's** assembly. Distinguish between singular and plural:

   SINGULAR: one **day's** work, a **month's** delay, a **dollar's** worth
   PLURAL: several **days'** work, three **months'** salary, two **dollars** worth

FINER POINTS

When a word ends with an *-s* that is not a plural *s*, people may add the possessive *-s* if they add an *s* in pronunciation: (both right) **Charles'** job or **Charles's** job.

PROBLEM SPOTTER

What was the problem in each sentence? How has it been resolved?

NO: The men's hand was cut and bleeding.
YES: The man's hand was cut and bleeding.
NO: Our societies shortcomings are endlessly debated.
YES: Our society's shortcomings are endlessly debated.
NO: The new Popes' goals were not yet known.
YES: The new Pope's goals were not yet known.
NO: The defendants twelve lawyer's total fees were astronomical.
YES: The defendant's twelve lawyers' total fees were astronomical.
NO: It could have been anyones mistake.
YES: It could have been anyone's mistake.

INSTANT REVIEW

Put a check mark next to each sentence that is satisfactory.

1 Both families' distant relatives had come for the occasion.   _____

2 The womans hockey team was still very new.   _____

3 Jose's grades have improved since last semester.   _____

4 The nation's economy had recovered from the recession.   _____

5 The union members strike vote had been postponed.   _____

6 The new dean was the Chemistry Department's first choice.   _____

7 Many cities budgets were hurt by the court decision.   _____

8 The book contrasted men's and women's styles of communication.   _____

9 Their monthly check paid for three week's worth of groceries.   _____

10 Somebody's mistake cost the company thousands of dollars.   _____

Name _____

EDITING PRACTICE

Enter the number of the right choice at the right.

1   My 1)family's/2)families' home was burglarized last week. _____

2   This 1)mornings/2)morning's paper brought bad news. _____

3   Both 1)company's/2)companies' stock had gone up. _____

4   Mark 1)Twains/2)Twain's books were read around the world. _____

5   Much of their 1)countrys/2)country's oil supply was gone. _____

6   1)Peoples/2)People's fears are forgotten in the face of danger. _____

7   1)Women's/2)Womens' apparel for office wear changed. _____

8   1)Office workers/2)Office worker's spent hours at the keyboard. _____

9   It is 1)nobodies/2)nobody's business what mail you receive. _____

10   1)Todays/2)Today's executives must understand tax law. _____

11   The last car in the line is 1)hers/2)her's. _____

12   1)Murphys/2)Murphy's Department Store is closing. _____

13   1)Yesterdays/2)Yesterday's announcement surprised everyone. _____

14   Football 1)player's/2)players no longer received scholarships. _____

15   The two sister 1)cities/2)city's were 1,200 miles apart. _____

16   The fish were wrapped in last 1)weeks/2)week's newspapers. _____

17   The 1)Hansen's/2)Hansens' house had long been for sale. _____

18   No one 1)elses/2)else's e-mail was being checked. _____

19   Your certificate came, but we never received 1)our's/2)ours. _____

20   The 1)governments/2)government's lawyers took on Microsoft. _____

INSTANT REWRITE

Rewrite the following passage, punctuating all possessives correctly as well as correcting misused apostrophes.

Play Ball

In many of the nations colleges, football player's have become the countries newest endangered species. As the spotted owls habitat is threatened by the loggers chainsaws, so many football players scholarships are endangered by the governments insistence on parity for womens sports. A young womans participation in sports will be as important as a young mans. No longer will one coachs salary equal three instructors income. Everyones health will benefit from an average students increased active participation instead of spectators just being couch potato's. Mens football and womens soccer will both attract large crowd's.

_____

_____

_____

_____

_____

_____

_____

_____

_____

_____

_____

_____

_____

_____

_____

_____

_____

_____

_____

CAPSULE RULE Use the apostrophe in the shortened or telescoped words called *contractions.*

Frequent use of contractions will make your writing seem informal. Contractions are fine in journal writing, in e-mail, in personal letters, and in accounts of personal experience. However, don't overuse them in writing that deals with issues and information. Maybe use only an occasional **don't, doesn't, isn't,** or **can't.** (Some instructors, and some style sheets for research reports and the like, rule out contractions altogether.) If you do use contractions, be very careful about their spelling.

1 Use the apostrophe to show where part of a word has been left out. Look especially for words combined with a shortened form of **not.** Look at where exactly the apostrophe goes in contractions like (cannot) **can't,** (is not) **isn't,** (are not) **aren't,** (has not) **hasn't,** (I will) **I'll,** and (will not) **won't.** Double-check the most predictable sources of problems: (do not) **don't,** (does not) **doesn't.**

BUILDING THE HABIT

Read the examples in the following set over several times.

CONTRACTIONS: that **can't** be right; they **don't** care; we **won't** yield; it **doesn't** work that way; they **shouldn't** do that; **we'll** correct the error; trains **hadn't** come through here in years; it **isn't** worth it

2 Distinguish between sound-alikes. Know how to tell apart **they're, their,** and **there.** Watch for pairs like **you're** and **your, who's** and **whose.**

BUILDING THE HABIT

Read the examples in the following set over several times.

▪ **They're** means **they are. Their** means it belongs to them. (There is also **there,** as in here and **there.**)

They're proud of **their** team.

▪ **Who's** means **who is. Whose** tells us to whom something belongs.

Who's the person **whose** car was towed?

▪ **You're** means **you are. Your** means it belongs to you.

You're entitled to **your** opinion.

▪ **We're** means **we are. Were** points to the past.

We're not what we **were.**

3 Avoid the *it's* trap. **It's** means **it is: it's** too late; **it's** not your fault; **it's** our second choice. **It's** also means **it has: it's** been raining. **Its** (without the apostrophe) means belonging to

157

it or related to it: the truck and **its** driver; the company and **its** suppliers; the jury and **its** verdict.

When you use *it's* and use it wrong, it shows in your writing as the most conspicuous spelling error in America today. The safest course is not to use *it's* (with the apostrophe) at all. Use **it is** when you mean it is. (Or use **it has** when you mean it has.) Otherwise use **its** (no apostrophe).

it is/its: **It is** the band's first stop on **its** road trip.
                   Its fans follow the band when **it is** on the road.

PROBLEM SPOTTER

What was the problem in each sentence? How has it been solved?

NO: Computer programs are'nt always compatible.
YES: **Computer programs aren't always compatible.**
NO: The band frequently changed it's schedule.
YES: **The band frequently changed its schedule.**
NO: Whose bringing suit against the company?
YES: **Who's bringing suit against the company?**
NO: Hes trying to build a model cathedral.
YES: **He's trying to build a model cathedral.**
NO: Their moving to Missouri at the end of the year.
YES: **They're moving to Missouri at the end of the year.**

BUILDING THE HABIT

Let the right spellings sink in. Read the sample sentences over several times.

1   We **can't** and **won't** close down the shelter.
2   **You're** on **your** own now.
3   What they **don't** know **doesn't** hurt them.
4   **They're** always **there** waving **their** signs.
5   She **hasn't** come in, so the report **isn't** ready.
6   **We're** often **where** we shouldn't be.
7   It **didn't** matter then and **doesn't** matter now.
8   **We'll** find out if **she's** right.
9   **It's** the first program of the institute at **its** new location.
10 **Who's** to say **whose** fault it is?

INSTANT REVIEW

Put a check mark after each sentence without a spelling problem.

Protect the Rain Forests

1   We can't let the tropical rain forests disappear.   _____
2   They're sheltering thousands of animal species.   _____
3   The forest dosen't just provide lumber for builders.   _____
4   Monkeys, birds, and snakes live in it's branches.   _____
5   Native tribes still live in its farthest reaches.   _____
6   Settlers cut and burn trees around there homesteads.   _____
7   Environmentalists dont approve of the slash-and-burn policy.   _____
8   Wholesale destruction isn't necessary.   _____
9   Who's to blame?   _____
10 Governments who's peasants want land need new policies.   _____

Name _____

EDITING PRACTICE

For each misspelled word, enter the corrected spelling on the right.

1   Whose the new prime minister?   _____

2   Many motorists didnt observe the speed limits.   _____

3   The bank announced it's new interest rate.   _____

4   Your not eligible for the student loans.   _____

5   Weve already notified the local police.   _____

6   Modern medical miracles are'nt cheap.   _____

7   We wont be able to stop the warming trend.   _____

8   Workers turn bitter when their laid off.   _____

9   The disease dosen't have a cure.   _____

10 Citizens cant usually sue their government.   _____

11 The newspaper was trying to build it's circulation.   _____

12 The homeless have disappeared from the news but their still with us. _____

13 The FBI could'nt stop serial killers but was monitoring chat rooms.   _____

14 When the computer crashes, your consulting the manual too late.   _____

15 It's never too late to send you're apology.   _____

16 The airline told its frequent flyers there mileage credits would expire. _____

17 The center opened it's exhibition devoted to early immigrants.   _____

18 The peregrine falcon wasnt considered endangered anymore.   _____

19 It's the first time the museum has'nt opened its doors on the holiday. _____

20 An earlier warning wouldve saved lives.   _____

INSTANT REWRITE

One way to minimize spelling problems caused by contractions is to use fewer of them. Look for contractions in the following passage. Change all contractions to the complete unshortened forms, and correct any remaining spelling problems.

Our group had planned it's trip for years. However, the timing couldnt have been worse. We've been told that the wild animal park hadnt had a worse tourist season during its existence. It's not often that years of drought deprive the animals of there water supply. Even so, we've learned much about the park and it's wildlife. Male elephants usually dont travel with their herd. It's surprising that female lions cant get males to do more of the hunting. It's been difficult for the local authorities to keep poachers out of the park.

_____

_____

_____

_____

_____

_____

_____

_____

_____

_____

_____

_____

_____

_____

_____

_____

_____

_____

_____

_____

_____

CAPSULE RULE Double-check both text on your computer screen and hard copy for damaging spelling errors.

Spellchecks today will alert you to most predictable spelling errors. They will also alert you to check for confusing words or for doubles that are often misspelled. You then have to decide which is the right choice for what you are saying. Check everything you print out or send out for the most common spelling demons.

1 Read the following list over and over again. These are the true "unforgivables." If you are a poor speller, pin this list up by your computer. A single *receive* or *definite* misspelled will hurt your credibility as a writer.

UNFORGIVABLES: receive, definite, perform, separate, occurred, athlete, surprise, dependent, basically, similar

2 Check carefully for *confusing pairs* of soundalikes: **their/there**; **accept/except**; **affect/effect**; **to/too**.

BUILDING THE HABIT

If confusing pairs give you trouble, read the following sets over several times:

- **their** shows belonging or possession; **there** shows location or starts *there is/there are* sentences:

    THEIR: they and **their** friends; people and **their** dogs; travelers with **their** luggage; stores and **their** customers

    THERE: here and **there**; we left it **there**; be **there** at eight; **there are** few lakes here; **there is** little hope

- **accept** means taking something on or taking it *in*; **except** means taking something *out*, making an exception:

    ACCEPT: I **accepted** the job; we will not **accept** responsibility; her resignation was **accepted**; an **acceptance** speech

    EXCEPT: the rules **excepted** senior citizens; present company **excepted**; we made no **exceptions**

- **affect** means a *limited* change; **effect** points to the *whole* result:

    AFFECT: it **affected** my grade; the chemical **affects** people's health; his worries have **affected** his performance

    EFFECT: the treatment had no **effect**; the skin showed the **effects** of radiation; an **effective** cure; the new management **effected** radical changes

- **to** shows direction (**to** school) or goes with the plain form of verbs (ready **to** study); **too** signals something excessive (**too** much of something) or it stands for also (that **too**):

    TO: **to** Europe, a trip **to** Havana, come **to** the table; eager **to** talk, reluctant **to** comply

    TOO: **too** late, **too** tired, **too** disillusioned, **too** much work

Other confusing pairs include **here** (opposite of there)/**hear** (listen); **council** (a group)/**counsel** (an advisor); **conscious** (aware)/**conscience** (our moral sense); **stationary** (standing still)/**stationery** (paper for letters); **principal** (head person or initial capital)/**principle** (firm standard or key idea).

3 Know the different spellings of *closely related words*. Pairs like the following show an important spelling change as you go from one use of the same root word to another: **personal** (belonging to that person)/**personnel** (the persons together making up the staff); **conscience** (moral sense)/**conscientious** (following your moral sense).

BUILDING THE HABIT

Study the changes in the following pairs. If you have trouble with words like these, read the examples over several times:

curious / **curiosity**	proceed / **procedure**
generous / **generosity**	dissent / **dissension**
courteous / **courtesy**	absorb / **absorption**
genius / **ingenious**	pronounce / **pronunciation**
fourteen / **forty**	till / **until**

Remember contrasts like the following:

we choose and lead (in the present)	we **chose** and **led** (in the past)
one hero, veto, potato	several **heroes, vetoes, potatoes**
one man, one woman	several **men**, several **women**
bigger than, more recent than	now and **then**, until **then**
no use for, an old prejudice	**used** to be, being **prejudiced**

Never write *of* instead of *have* in sentences like the following: I **could have sworn** it was you. (Not: I *could of* sworn.) There **should have been** more. (Not: There *should of* been.)

4 Watch changing uses of the **hyphen.** Hyphenated words are a halfway house between words that are completely separate (*guard dog*) and completely blended (*guardrail*). Many words habitually used together are spelled like a **single word** (*headache, grandfather, gunfire, guesswork*). Others are still **separate**—two words (*first lady, high school, country club, blood bank*). But many others are in between and joined by a hyphen. Study groups of typical examples:

1 sister-in-law, mother-in-law, in-laws, great-grandfather
2 first-rate, six-pack, one-sided, one-way
3 Spanish-speaking, law-abiding, award-winning
4 dark-haired, air-conditioned, middle-aged, foreign-born
5 fuel-efficient, cost-effective, water-repellent, toll-free
6 two-by-four, south-southeast, fly-by-night, cash-and-carry
7 drive-in, teach-in, take-off, off-season, by-laws

Study basic rules for hyphenation:

- Hyphenate **compound** (combined) numbers from **twenty-one** to **ninety-nine.**
- Use the hyphen with the introductory tags (**prefixes**) *all-*, *self-*, and *ex-* (in the sense of "former"). But make **coauthor** and **prewar** single words.

  all-: all-knowing, all-purpose, all-embracing
  self-: self-conscious, self-confident, self-contained, self-explanatory
  ex-: ex-champion, ex-senator, ex-husband, ex-mayor

- Use a hyphen when the prefix comes before a word that starts with a *capital* letter: **pro-Arab, un-American, anti-British, non-Catholic.**
- Use the hyphen with **group modifiers**—several words that take the place of a single word to tell us what kind: **easy-to-follow** directions.

  HYPHENS: You can dial station to station. We placed a **station-to-station call.**
  The program had twelve steps. It was a **twelve-step program.**

- Formerly hyphenated Americans now often prefer *no hyphen:* **Mexican American, African Americans, Polish American.**

Name _____

PROBLEM SPOTTER

What was the problem in each sentence? How has it been resolved?

NO: The course focused on oral English and pronounciation.
YES: **The course focused on oral English and pronunciation.**
NO: They tried to use a step by step approach.
YES: **They tried to use a step-by-step approach.**
NO: It's true that frequent absences can effect your grade.
YES: **It's true that frequent absences can affect your grade.**
NO: Several colleges excepted her application.
YES: **Several colleges accepted her application.**
NO: She placed twenty first in a field of forty five candidates.
YES: **She placed twenty-first in a field of forty-five candidates.**

INSTANT REVIEW

Put a check mark next to each sentence that is satisfactory.

1   Many people are prejudice against change.   _____

2   They fear changes in there customs or traditions.   _____

3   This change of plans will affect everyone in the company.   _____

4   His conscience would not allow him to keep the money.   _____

5   Class schedules use to be available months in advance.   _____

6   Their all-knowing attitude made it difficult to like them.   _____

7   The new management adopted a dog eat dog attitude.   _____

8   The new procedures were hard to implement.   _____

9   She was to self-conscious to go up on the stage.   _____

10 A coworker accepted the award on their behalf.   _____

EDITING PRACTICE 1

In each of the following sentences a word has been left incomplete. Enter the completed word on the right.

1   The host _____cepted my apologies.   _____

2   The princip_____ of the school believed in discipline.   _____

3   Some English sounds are difficult for the Vietnamese to pron_____. _____

4   The adverse health _____fects of smoking are well known.   _____

5   The English at one time were prejudic_____ against the Irish.   _____

6   The military academies began to enroll wom_____.   _____

7   A blight affecting potat_____ caused the famine.   _____

8   The operators were use_____ to surveillance.   _____

9   Everyone voted for the measure _____cept Georgio.   _____

10 The ruling _____fected mainly older employees.   _____

EDITING PRACTICE 2

Which groups of words need hyphens? Enter the hyphenated combinations on the line below each sentence.

1   User friendly software programs need easy to follow directions.

2   Her middle aged friend was a dyed in the wool conservative.

3   The self confident candidate was the ex mayor of a fast growing city.

4   The editor of the English language newspaper was accused of pro Arab views.

6   His Spanish speaking relatives had mixed feelings about their all American cousin.

7   Get rich quick schemes are promoted by fly by night operators.

8   Sit ins and teach ins had been part of the end the war movement.

9   Cancer causing factors had been ignored by business as usual executives.

10   We must find more fuel efficient, cost effective means of transportation.

11   A flabby middle aged two pack a day smoker became a 160 pound marathon runner.

12   He was a law and order candidate who promised to crack down on ex convicts.

13   The Connecticut based subsidiary produces computer aided high performance robots for state of the art factories.

14   Few self respecting candidates conduct old fashioned campaigns taking them to out of the way places.

15   The ex ambassador complained about anti American demonstrations.

Spelling rules help you focus on groups of words that cause similar spelling problems. The rules are rough guides with exceptions, but they bring together groups of words that you can study together. Look them over, spell them out, write them out. Come back to them for review till the right spellings become second nature.

1   First rule: Remember that English spelling is only partly phonetic. (It only partly reproduces the sounds of current speech.) Include the **missing letters** in words misspelled because of sounds often not clearly heard: lib**r**ary, Feb**r**uary, busi**n**ess, gove**rn**ment, de**b**t, fore**ig**n, qua**n**tity, proba**b**ly, enviro**n**ment, basica**ll**y, accide**nt**ally. Watch for **a lot** and **no one** (two words) and **nevertheless** (one).

2   Remember the **i-before-e** rule. For the long *ee* sound in words like *believe* or *retrieve*, put the *i* before the *e*—except after a *c*. Remember: It's bel**ie**ve (**ie**) but rece**i**ve (**cei**). If you have trouble with these, read each set over several times:

ie: ach**ie**ve, bel**ie**ve, ch**ie**f, n**ie**ce, p**ie**ce (of pie), rel**ie**ve
cei: c**ei**ling, conc**ei**ted, conc**ei**ve, perc**ei**ve, rec**ei**ve, rec**ei**pt
EXCEPTIONS: (*ei*) **ei**ther, l**ei**sure, n**ei**ther, s**ei**ze, w**ei**rd; (*cie*) finan**cie**r, spe**cie**s

3   Watch out for **doubled consonants.** Vowels are *a, e, i, o, u,* and some of their combinations—sounds easy to sound out by themselves. Other sounds that go with them are consonants, like *b, c, g,* or *n.*

   ■ Double a single consonant at the end of the word if you add an ending like *-ed, -er,-est, -ing.* Each of these added endings starts with a vowel: plan-pla**nn**ed-pla**nn**ing; big-bi**gg**er-bi**gg**est.

   ■ The doubled consonant must follow a short, single vowel that is also **stressed** (or accented)—standing out in pronunciation: ad**mit**-ad**mit**ted-ad**mit**ting; be**gin**-be**ginn**ing. It's re**fer**-re**ferr**ed-re**ferr**ing—but *no* doubling in **ref**erence (the stress has shifted away from the end).

   ■ There is no doubling of the consonant after a long or double vowel like *oa, ee,* or the *o* in *hope* and *cope*: seed-see**d**ing; boat-boa**t**ing, hope-hop**i**ng (not *hopping*).

BUILDING THE HABIT

   If you have trouble with doubled consonants, read each of the following sets over several times:

DOUBLING: plan-planned , stop-stopped-stoppage, red-redder, ban-banned-banning, trip-tripped
DOUBLING: begin-beginning, prefer-preferred, occurred-occurrence
NO DOUBLING: refer-reference, prefer-preference, hate-hating, benefit-benefited edit-edited-editing

4   Watch for changing endings of words like *study, city,* and *family.* Change the **single -y** at the end of the word to *ie* if you add the *-s* ending: she stud**ies**; two cit**ies**, our famil**ies**. Change the final *y* to *i* before other endings (beauty/beautiful). However, leave it unchanged before *-ing:* study**ing**, copy**ing**.

BUILDING THE HABIT

   If you have trouble with words like **families** (not *familys*) and **studying** (not *studing*), read each of the following sets over several times:

ie: family-families, fly-flies, study-studies, try-tries, quantity-quantities, copy-copied, dry-drier, noisy-noisily

i: duty-dutiful, deny-denial, busy-business, noisy-noisily

y: copying, studying, trying, worrying

Keep the *y* if it is part of a double vowel: del**ays**, pl**ays**, enj**oys**. (Exceptions: day-d**ai**ly, say-s**ai**d, pay-p**ai**d, gay-g**ai**ly)

FINER POINTS

When you use the possessive form of words like *family* and *city*, make sure to spell singular and plural differently:

SINGULAR: one family and the **family's** friends; one city and the **city's** borders

PLURAL: two families and the **families'** friends; two cities and the **cities'** borders

5 Drop a silent **final -e** if you add an ending that begins with a vowel: bore-**boring** (but boredom), like-**liking** and **likable** (but likely), hate-**hating** (but hateful), love-**loving** and **lovable** (but lovely). Exceptions are the endings *-ge* and *-ce*. They remain unchanged in words like **advantageous, changeable, courageous,** or **noticeable.** There are also other exceptions:

EXCEPTIONS: argue-**argument**, due-**duly**, dye-**dyeing** (coloring), mile-**mileage**, true-**truly**, whole-**wholly, salable** but also **saleable**

6 For words like the following, look for a **tie-in** with a related word:

definite (finish)	permissible (permissive)	confident (confidential)
separate (separation)	existence (existential)	brilliant (brilliance)
dispensable (dispensary)	attendant (attendance)	

PROBLEM SPOTTER

What was the problem in each of the following sentences? How was the problem resolved?

NO: Similar accidents had occured the year before.

YES: **Similar accidents had occurred the year before.**

NO: The sister citys mayors had met for a festive banquet.

YES: **The sister cities' mayors had met for a festive banquet.**

NO: Students could invite only members of their immediate familys.

YES: **Students could invite only members of their immediate families.**

NO: The scholarships had basicly gone to male athletes.

YES: **The scholarships had basically gone to male athletes.**

NO: The college offered incentives to students studing abroad.

YES: **The college offered incentives to students studying abroad.**

INSTANT REVIEW

Put a check mark after each sentence without a spelling problem.

1 The student goverment voted in favor of a multicultural center. _____

2 The librarian at the reference desk had always been helpful. _____

3 The mayor referred all inquirys to the Public Relations Officer. _____

4 The ads promised truly amazing mileage. _____

5 Most of the preppies preferred studying at night. _____

6 The FBI commited inadequate resources to the task. _____

7 The referal had been misdirected to the wrong office. _____

8 The students' families tried to stop worrying. _____

9 In the begining minority students kept to themselves. _____

10 By February we had still not received a definite answer. _____

Name _____

EDITING PRACTICE
In the following sentences, combine the two parts of each incomplete word.

1   It would have been more 1)advantage + ous to rely   _____
    2)sole + ly on our own resources.   _____

2   If he had been less 1)conc—ted + ie or ei, he could   _____
    have 2)perc—ved + ie or ei his own faults.   _____

3   The council could have 1)stop + ed the disturbances   _____
    by 2)prohibit + ing all public gatherings.   _____

4   1)Busy + ness has been much better since we started   _____
    2)copy + ing the methods of our competitors.   _____

5   We 1)regret+ ed that we had not thought of stating   _____
    our 2)prefer + ence earlier.   _____

6   Our efforts have not made the place 1)beauty +ful,   _____
    but we have 2)try + ed.   _____

7   Though none of the players were 1)permit + ed to   _____
    leave, there were 2)notice + able exceptions.   _____

8   Defense 1)industry + s had found the low-cost,   _____
    nonunion area to their 2)like + ing.   _____

9   No one 1)bel—ved + ie or ei that a professional   _____
    wrestler could 2)rec—ve + ei or ie enough votes.   _____

10 The relatives were 1)noisy + ly celebrating the   _____
    reconciliation of the two 2)family + s.   _____

11 We had 1)rec—ved + ie or ei only two offers   _____
    since the 2)bid + ing started.   _____

12 By 1)create + ing a planning commission, the   _____
    county solved some 2)unmanage + able problems.   _____

13 A 1)begin + er needs to learn that almost any paper   _____
    can be improved by careful 2)edit + ing.   _____

14   When we last 1)pay + ed them a visit, we all went to a   _____

      2)bore + ing play.   _____

15   A similar 1)occur + ence had disrupted a cultural   _____

      event in the twin 2)city + s.   _____

16   The manager always said he was 1)delay + ed when   _____

      he could have simply 2)admit + ed that he was late.   _____

17   1)N—ther + ie or ei the skipper nor the others   _____

      thought we were 2)courage + ous enough to join the crew.   _____

18   The play 1)imply + s that those who   _____

      2)defy + ed the government obeyed a higher law.   _____

19   We were 1)hope +ing for speedy approval of the   _____

      project, but someone 2)interfere + ed.   _____

20   We were 1)hope + ing we could secure the   _____

      necessary 2)quantity + s at a reasonable price.   _____

CAPSULE RULE Capitalize names as well as *I* and first words in a sentence.

1 Capitalize **proper names**—the names of individual people, things, groups, places, institutions. Some words are always proper names and therefore always capitalized: The**Mormons** moved to **Utah** from the **Midwest** and built **Salt Lake City.**

PEOPLE:	Hillary Clinton, Eleanor Roosevelt, Billy Graham
LOCATIONS:	Dallas, Texas, United States, England, Cuba, North America
INSTITUTIONS:	Hoover Institute, Mills College, University of Michigan
RELIGIONS:	Jewish, Catholic, Greek Orthodox, Islam
NAMES ON MAPS:	the Mississippi, the Atlantic, the Panama Canal
VESSEL OR CRAFT:	the *Apollo*, the *Mayflower*, the *California Zephyr*

Capitalize the names of days and months but not of the seasons: **Monday** and **July** but *spring* and *fall.*

2 Especially capitalize labels of **languages and nationalities,** such as **English, Filipino, Arab, Israeli.**

LANGUAGE OR ETHNICITY: Spanish, Mexican, Japanese, American, Chinese, Polish, African American, Latino, Italian, Hebrew, Vietnamese

3 Capitalize **labels using proper names.** For instance, capitalize religions named after their founders and also ideas or products named after their inventors: **Lutherans, Buddhism, Marxist** economics, **Freudian** psychology.

BASED ON NAMES: **Buddhist** monastery, **Copernican** universe, **Freudian** psychology, **Christian** civilization

4 Always capitalize the **first word** of a sentence and the word *I:* **He** told me **I** was his best friend.

BACKUP EXPLANATION

- Capitalize titles or words like *street* and *avenue* when they become **parts** of a proper name: **Senator Feinstein, Mayor Garret, Broad Street, Pennsylvania Avenue, Sister Mary Elizabeth, Mount Rushmore.**
- Some words work both ways—both as general terms (lower case) and as specific labels (capitalized). We have many **democratic** institutions (lower case) but only one **Democratic** party (capitalized proper name). Our country is a **republic**—no king or dictator (lower case) and we have a **Republican** party.
  When you say "**my mother**—not your mother" or "**my father**—not your father," you are referring to a general relationship (lower case—everyone had a mother). But you use capitals when you say "**Mother** quarreled with **Father** till **Grandmother** told them to stop" (these are the people you but no one outside your family calls by these names).
- Capitalize the words in titles of **publications** and your own papers: **The Trouble** with **Ethnic Humor.** However, do *not* capitalize connecting words like **articles** (*the, a, an*),

prepositions (*at, in, with, for, by, with, without*), and **coordinators** (*and, but, for*) unless they are the first or last word of a title.

TITLES: The Wizard of Oz, Life among the Highland Gorillas, Flying High without a Parachute

FINER POINTS

Longer prepositions—*among, without, around*—are now treated like other prepositions—lower case, *not* capitalized.

PROBLEM SPOTTER

What was the problem in each of the following sentences? How was it resolved?

NO: They were planning to visit taos, new mexico, and several navaho reservations.
YES: **They were planning to visit Taos, New Mexico, and several Navaho reservations.**
NO: Studying chinese is much more difficult than studying languages more closely related to english, such as spanish or german.
YES: **Studying Chinese is much more difficult than studying languages more closely related to English, such as Spanish or German.**
NO: The film festival at richmond college screens classics like *gone with the wind.*
YES: **The film festival at Richmond College screens classics like *Gone with the Wind.***
NO: Next tuesday, general electric will hold interviews at west valley community college.
YES: **Next Tuesday, General Electric will hold interviews at West Valley Community College.**
NO: The evening classes enrolled a cross-section of filipino, korean, pakistani, mexican, and nicaraguan students.
YES: **The evening classes enrolled a cross-section of Filipino, Korean, Pakistani, Mexican, and Nicaraguan students.**

INSTANT REVIEW

In which of the following sentences are all words capitalized correctly? Put a check mark on the right for each satisfactory sentence.

1   Students at American high schools study French or Spanish, but few learn Chinese.   _____

2   Every summer, Aunt Audrey dreaded vacations because my brother and I always argued.   _____

3   Jeffrey took swimming lessons on monday and wednesday mornings.   _____

4   Of all the parks, they liked Yellowstone and Yosemite the best.   _____

5   The europeans started to imitate theme parks like Disneyland and Great America.   _____

6   Each Spring, photographers come to Washington, D.C., to take pictures of the cherry blossoms.   _____

7   Comparative religion studies christian, jewish, and Muslim thought.   _____

8   Pope John Paul II has traveled to countries including Poland, Cuba, and Brazil.   _____

9   Fewer students were taking latin, german, or russian.   _____

10   People from the middle west and the east coast envied the casual attitude of Californians.   _____

Name _____

EDITING PRACTICE

Suppose because of a malfunction your computer did not print out capital letters. Supply the missing capitalization. Below each sentence, write all the words that should be capitalized.

1   the supreme court may reverse the decisions of lower courts.

_____

2   modern democracy traces its root to early greek thinkers.

_____

3   they discussed whether an aquarius could be happy with a libra.

_____

4   many americans bought books about corporate success, such as *in search of excellence.*

_____

5   the sequoia national forest was closed during last summer's fire warning.

_____

6   the new american ambassador to egypt was familiar with egyptian history and customs.

_____

7   my grandparents came to america from italy the year theodore roosevelt sent troops to cuba.

_____

8   corporations like nike announced new policies concerning child labor in southeast asia.

_____

9   during world war two, the united states joined england and france after the december bombing of pearl harbor.

_____

10 many vietnamese families living in colorado or california still celebrate the vietnamese new year with traditional foods and festivities.

_____

PROOFREADING PRACTICE

Proofread the following paper for missing or misused capitals but also for missing or misused apostrophes and hyphens. Cross out each misspelled word and write the corrected word above the line.

Prison reform uses many different approaches. Countries like spain, israel, denmark, and the united states have many different ways of rehabilitating prisoners. People in canada wanted to see more inmates working in or for the community. alberta, canada, opened offices instead of jails, steering convicts into community work rather than prison. At a forest camp at shulie lake, nova scotia, scott paper employed convicts on jobs others would not take. In ontario, canada, on a typical day groups were out cleaning parks, shoveling snow, or caring for disabled children.

Germany also has tried a different approach to rehabilitation. Inmates of a prison in hamburg participated in an experiment letting hardcore offenders be part of a crew aboard the greek schooner *yachara*. They performed all duties of a crew for a week long voyage on the baltic sea.

Spain tried a loosely structured prison for women. A womens prison in madrid let the prisoners run the cultural and recreational programs by themselves. Inmates were able to receive visitors and had the right of unrestricted communication with their families.

Prisons in the United States have tried many different reforms. One solution is similar to one of Israels experiments. Morgantown, west virginia, divided offenders into four behavioral categories. Some prisons in the united states became partly self supporting through the federal prison industries, inc. This organization was set up to provide vocational training for inmates.

I believe we should make more of an all out effort to improve the current system. This point was strongly made in an off Broadway play about prison life written by an ex convict. Publications like *the new republic* and *harper's* have long shown a strong interest in prison reform.

ESL—ENGLISH AS A SECOND CULTURE

1 YOUR LANGUAGE HISTORY If English is your second language, what was your first? How much do you know about your first language? Where is it spoken? By what kind of people? What is their history? Tell your classmates from a different language background about your first language. The following is a possible model for your **language history:**

Spanish is a world language spoken by an estimated 352 million people. It is the official language of more countries around the world than any other language except English. It is the language of Spain, the mother country, and it is the official language of Mexico and Cuba and other countries of Central America. It is the language of Puerto Rico and of the countries of South America except Brazil. Spain was for centuries a trading nation with a far-flung colonial empire spanning the seas. Spanish conquistadors and missionaries brought the Spanish language to the Americas and to the Philippines. Spanish originally was an offshoot of the Latin language that the Romans brought to Spain when Spain was part of the Roman empire. This explains why Spanish-speaking Americans have started to call themselves *Latinos* (for men) or *Latinas* (for women). There are regional differences in pronunciation and word choice between the Spanish spoken in different countries, as there are in English. However, people who speak Spanish can make themselves understood in widely different areas of the Spanish-speaking world.

_____

_____

_____

_____

_____

_____

_____

_____

_____

_____

_____

_____

_____

_____

_____

2 LANGUAGE AND ATTITUDES   People learning a new language are also learning different attitudes or differing values. Learning another language means more than just translating words from one language to another. For instance, the way things are said in one language may sound impolite or aggressive in another. Calling a new acquaintance by the first name may seem very rude. Read the following **case history** of one newcomer's "culture shock." For your classmates, write an account of your own experiences with different attitudes or values you encountered when learning to use English as a second language.

CASE HISTORY:

An immigrant from mainland China now teaches English in an American two-year college. He reports that in China he was taught to use *we* instead of *I* when he stated opinions. Using *I* made people sound selfish and individualistic. It made them sound self-centered and self-promoting, like people in bourgeois (middle-class or capitalistic) countries who looked out only for themselves. He remembers propaganda posters that said "Down with the word *I!*" and "Trust the masses!" Even when he stated his own opinions, he tried hard to present them as the views of people in authority or of the party leaders. In this country, he had to invent for himself a new "English self." He had to learn to write in a way that at home would have sounded boastful or disrespectful of authority. For a long time, the words *self* and *individual* still had negative associations in his mind. He slowly changed from his old timid, humble, modest Chinese identity to a more confident, assertive, and aggressive American self.

_____

_____

_____

_____

_____

_____

_____

_____

_____

_____

_____

_____

_____

_____

_____

_____

Name _____

TESTING YOUR CULTURAL LITERACY

To understand what people are saying, you need to know what their words mean in the culture in which they live. The following questions test your **cultural literacy**—your under-standing of what educated people in this country might talk about. Put a check mark next to the right answer.

1 Where are negative test results good news?
  a in the doctor's office _____
  b in the principal's office _____
2 Which sentence has real birds in it?
  a We killed two birds with one stone. _____
  b Condors are making a comeback. _____
3 When you are looking for a new hard drive,
  a you are looking for an easier commute _____
  b you are shopping for equipment for your computer _____
4 Priests who are celibate
  a remain unmarried _____
  b have to live in a monastery _____
5 An epic is
  a an illness spreading quickly everywhere _____
  b a long poem about heroes and great deeds _____
6 When we commemorate the war dead
  a we bury them in a common cemetery _____
  b we make sure their sacrifice is remembered _____
7 When you illuminate a stadium
  a you are turning on bright lights _____
  b you are closing it down _____
8 Matrimony is another word for
  a marriage _____
  b constant quarreling _____
9 Fiasco is the word for
  a a well-known American soft drink _____
  b an undertaking that turns into a disaster _____
10 The temperance movement
  a pioneered air conditioning _____
  b fought against alcohol abuse _____
11 A dialogue is
  a a verbal exchange between two or more speakers _____
  b a regional variety of a language _____
12 Suffrage is another word for
  a a new generation of pain killers _____
  b the right to vote _____
13 Disinformation is
  a the same message sent for the second time _____
  b wrong information circulated on purpose _____
14 When Southern states seceded,
  a they left the Union _____
  b expanded westward _____

15 Abolition brought
    a the banning of marijuana
    b the end of slavery   ————
16 Velocity is
    a a physicist's term for speed
    b a biologist's term for rate of growth   ————
17 Polygamous societies allow people
    a to have more than one spouse
    b to worship more than one god   ————
18 People who start the day with a constitutional
    a start with a reading of the constitution
    b start with a workout   ————
19 People who look for the silver lining
    a buy only top-of-the-line clothes
    b look for something good in bad news   ————
20 When we rationalize, we
    a look for a rational answer
    b look for excuses   ————

THE WAY AMERICA TALKS

Newcomers to America have often identified the following as "typically American expressions." Which of these to you seems most typically American? Choose one of these for a **journal entry.** Where have you encountered the expression? What role does it play in the American experience? (Or choose an expression that to you is "typically American.")

"to start all over again"
"there is some good in everyone"
"smile and the world smiles with you"
"you win some; you lose some"
"nobody knows you when you're down and out"
"have a good day"
"you never know"

Are you prepared for the language needs of the world of work? Jobs vary greatly in how much verbal communication they require. However, in the age of the information highway and the knowledge explosion, more and more of the world's work means working with language. It means memos, reports, proposals, evaluations, queries, briefings and debriefings. How do you rank your language ability or proficiency in areas like the following?

▪ The *language of computers* is international, with many originally English terms now taken over into other languages. (Russian high school students work computer games dealing with the development of urban communities—with all the descriptions and instructions in English.) How much of the language of the computer world do you know? Is it enough to help you deal effectively with computer experts and computer needs? With which of the following terms are you comfortable or familiar? Which would you have to check out?

CYBERSPACE: online, software, cyberspace, CD-ROM, compatibility, hacker, file names, multimedia applications, pre-configured, pirating, Internet explorer, DOS, scanner, links, RAM, virus

GROUP WORK

If you can, discuss both easy and difficult terms with other second language learners.

▪ How much of the *language of modern business* do you know? How much would you need to understand if you came into an organization as a new employee? With which of the following terms are you comfortable or familiar? Which would you have to check out?

BUSINESS: flextime, temporaries, benefits, outsourcing, configuration, worker's compensation, middleman, patent infringement, shareholder value, anti-trust legislation, probationary employee, royalties, downsizing, lease-purchase

GROUP WORK

If you can, discuss both easy and difficult terms with other second language learners.

▪ How much of the *language of law* do you need to understand what might be involved in a lawsuit or what goes on in a court of law? With which of the following terms are you comfortable or familiar? Which would you have to check out?

LAW: litigation, liability, plaintiff, defendant, indictment, grand jury, court of appeals, felony, public defender, three strikes, plagiarism, recidivism, battery, culpability, conflict of interest, co-defendant, parole, subpoena, warrant

GROUP WORK

If you can, discuss both easy and difficult terms with other second language learners.

YOUR LANGUAGE INVENTORY

Choose *one* of the three areas—computers, business, or law. Write a **journal entry** discussing what you learned and how you learned about the language of the chosen field. Among the terms listed in this unit, choose for discussion some that gave you trouble but also others that you came to know well.

_____

_____

_____

_____

_____

_____

_____

_____

_____

_____

_____

_____

_____

_____

_____

_____

_____

_____

_____

_____

_____

_____

_____

_____

_____

Name _____

A QUICK-CHECK OF BUSINESS ENGLISH

How good are you at explaining to coworkers new expressions that they may not have heard before? Write **capsule definitions** of the following:

1 **EXAMPLE:** outsourcing
      **farming out business operations or manufacturing to outside firms,
      often with lower-paid worker**s

2 computer-literate

_____

_____

3 aptitude tests

_____

_____

4 the paperless office

_____

_____

5 the glass ceiling

_____

_____

6 focus groups

_____

_____

7 flextime

_____

_____

8 interactive

_____

_____

9 user-friendly

_____

_____

10 downsizing

_____

_____

11 multitasking

_____

_____

12 middle management

_____

_____

13 stock options

_____

_____

14 spellcheck

_____

_____

15 flow chart

_____

_____

16 deductibles

_____

_____

17 golden parachute

_____

_____

18 perks

_____

_____

19 termination

_____

_____

20 probationary employee

_____

_____

CAPSULE RULE   Pay special attention to how nouns are used in a sentence.

Nouns are everywhere in English sentences. We use them to point to people, things, ideas, actions, or conditions. Nouns are label words. For instance, all the names of products, tools, materials, birds, flowers, and trees are nouns: **lightbulb, chainsaw, board, blue jay, daffodil, oak.** All the names of types of vehicles and all the labels we use to classify people are nouns: **car, van, bus, truck; immigrant, clerk, athlete, teacher, nurse.** All the names of institutions, activities, and events are nouns: **college, hospital, competition, concert, holiday.**

To use the right form of a noun, check the number: *one or more?* Are you talking about just *one* person or one object or event (**singular**)? Or are you talking about *two or more* (**plural**)? The basic rule for normal or regular English nouns is: Add the *-s* ending to show more than one.

REGULAR PLURAL: **lightbulbs, chainsaws, boards, blue jays, daffodils, oaks; cars, vans, buses, trucks; immigrants, clerks, athletes, teachers, nurses**

Most English nouns follow this rule, including especially labels of activities, events, and ideas. Read all examples over several times:

REGULAR PLURAL: Beware of **imitations. Applications** are due Monday. No **refunds.** We are closed **Sundays.** They enjoyed their **vacations.** We accepted their **apologies.** The U.S. supported friendly **governments.**

However, some very common everyday nouns use an older method of making plurals. Instead of adding the ending, they make a change in the word itself:

IRREGULAR PLURALS: one **man**/several **men;** one **woman**/several **women;** one **child**/several **children;** one **tooth**/several **teeth;** one **foot**/several **feet;** one **freshman**/several **freshmen**

INSTANT REVIEW

Focus on all the changes in the following passage as it is changed from singular to plural. Read the second set over several times:

SINGULAR: A **man** and a **woman** may have **difficulty** when communicating. The **partner** in a **relationship** or a **marriage** may seem to come from a different **planet.** A **couple** may attend a **workshop** to help with the **problem.** Is the **man** too assertive? Is the **male** a poor **listener?** Is the **woman** too indirect, not spelling out a real **need** or **apprehension?** A **comedian** may make us laugh at this **situation.** When the **woman** talks about the **relationship,** does the **man** really think about an oil **change** for the **car?**

PLURAL: **Men** and **women** may have **difficulties** when communicating. The **partners** in **relationships** or **marriages** may seem to come from different **planets. Couples** may attend **workshops** to help with **problems.** Are **men** too assertive? Are **males** poor **listeners?** Are **women** too indirect, not spelling out real **needs** or **apprehensions? Comedians** may make us laugh at these **situations.** When **women** talk about **relationships,** do **men** really think about oil **changes** for their **cars?**

FINER POINTS

Not all English nouns use the -s plural, although the great majority does. Just a few use the plain or unmarked form for the plural:

UNMARKED PLURALS: several **people**, numerous **sheep**, fewer **deer**

Many other nouns are used only as singulars—with no plural form:

NO PLURALS: violence, television, prime time, sadness, wildlife, wrestling

EDITING PRACTICE

Fill in the right form of the noun in parentheses. Ask yourself: singular or plural?

The Violent Screens

Violence on the screen no longer just means a few fist (fight) _____ or an evening of

(wrestling) _____. In (dozen) _____ of Schwarzenegger (movie)

_____, the hero has killed several hundred (people) _____, making him

one of the top serial (killer) _____ of American (entertainment) _____.

Movie (producer) _____ have human (being) _____ killed off with fewer

(scruple) _____ than (other) _____ would have taking a dog to the

(pound) _____. Senseless (act) _____ of (violence) _____

occur in the many cop (show) _____ that are shown in (prime time)

_____. Some of the worst (offender) _____ are the makers of (program)

_____ aimed at small (child) _____. Millions of (youngster)

_____ watch countless (firing) _____ of (weapon) _____.

Animal cartoon (character) _____ administer violent (beating) _____ to

other creatures. I remember an early video (game) _____ where the player zapped

platoons of alien space (invader) _____. In some of today's worst (example)

_____, the player decapitates and disembowels a human (opponent)

_____.

Name _____

To use nouns right, study the signal words that often tell us a noun is about to follow. **Articles** are brief signal words that tell us: "Noun ahead!" Often the noun follows immediately: **the counselor, a relationship, the solution.** Often other material comes between the article and the noun: **the** experienced **counselor, a** troubled **relationship, a** perfect **solution.**

Nouns do not come with an article automatically attached. Instead you have to choose among three possibilities:

■ When do you use the **indefinite** article—**a** or **an** (**a** problem, **an** opportunity)? Things are still open or indefinite—you are not yet singling out one as different from any other. You are not closing in on one definite example as "this particular one":

INDEFINITE: **A car** blocked the driveway.
                (Who knows what or whose it is?)
                I need to pick **a** better **search engine.**
                (I have not yet picked one.)
                We were looking for **a police officer.**
                (At this point *any* officer would do.)
                We had **a quiz** every Friday.
                (At this point we are not looking at a particular one.)

■ When do you use the **definite** article—**the** (**the** central problem, **the** last opportunity)? You have definitely singled out one from many. When you say, "**The stranger** followed us," you are referring to one you had previously noticed or mentioned. You have focused on that particular one.

DEFINITE: There was no way to move **the car.** (that particular one)
              The landlord raised the rent. (this particular landlord)
              The number had been changed. (that particular number)
              The exam was all true-and-false. (this particular one)

Often the change from **a/an** to **the** shows a change from general to specific:

GENERAL: She opened **a magazine** and started to read **an article.**
              (could have been any—we don't know much about her choices)
SPECIFIC: She finished **the article** and put away **the magazine.**
              (By now we know which—the magazine and the article she picked earlier.)

■ Why do some nouns appear with **no article** at all? Something may not come in countable items but in bulk, like *water* or *fuel* or *cement*. Such a noun may be used not as a count noun but as a **bulk noun**—no article. Words for **general qualities** like *hope, happiness*, or *loyalty* work the same way:

NO ARTICLE: tread **water; food** for **thought** (not *the food for the thought*); pouring **concrete**
NO ARTICLE: giving up **hope**, finding **happiness**, rewarding **loyalty**

Even with bulk nouns, you will use the definite, specifying article **the** when you focus on a definite example. Read the following *contrasting pairs* over several times:

liking **rice** (generally)/not liking **the rice** (that came with this particular meal)
welcoming **advice** (usually)/rejecting **the advice** her lawyer gave (in this particular case)
buying **software** (unspecified)/installing **the software** (previously identified)

rewarding **effort** (as a general policy)/worrying about **the effort** needed to trace the records (in this particular case)

buying **furniture** (off and on)/moving **the furniture** (in this particular apartment)

With plural nouns, use **no article** when you talk about things in general—not specifying or singling out particular ones.

GENERAL: **Communities** need committed **teachers** and trained **doctors**, not more **lawyers**.
SPECIFIC: **The taxpayers** of this city need to send a message to **the supervisors**.

FINER POINTS

Watch for how articles are used with **proper names**—for instance, names of institutions, countries, rivers, oceans, or ships.

- It's **the FBI** and **the Pentagon** but often just **Congress** (or **the Congress** of the United States). It's **the University of Michigan** but **Evergreen Community College**.
- Countries usually appear without the article (in **Canada**, from **China**, to **Mexico**). However, there are important exceptions (in **the U.S.**, from **the United Kingdom**, in **the former Soviet Union**).

EDITING PRACTICE

In each blank space in a sentence, fill in the article **the** (for definite article) or **a/an** (for indefinite article). Or leave the space blank.

1 Her family had come from _____ Brazil to _____ United States.

2 The letter came from _____ president of the college.

3 His brother had played _____ football in high school.

4 When a car pulled up, they watched _____ vehicle carefully.

5 The manager played _____ golf in the afternoon.

6 When a solicitor rang the bell, the dog barked at _____ unwanted visitor.

7 They had _____ children but did not have _____ grandchild.

8 After voting on it, the legislature sent _____ bill to _____ governor.

9 Each application they received was from _____ highly qualified person.

10 Each country has _____ flag, as do individual states.

CAPSULE RULE   **Work on the verb forms that show your knowledge of English.**

Every language scholar or teacher knows there is a big difference between knowing something in theory and applying it in practice. If you use English as a second language, this is especially true for verbs—words we use in every sentence when talking about actions, activities, or conditions:

VERBS: The candidate **campaigned** hard. Internet sales **are booming.**
           The board had denied their request. The parking lot **was** full.

What do you need to watch for especially? Like the verbs in many other languages, English verbs show the listener what time it is. They change their forms for different timeframes, or **tenses:** It **rains** (now); it **rained** (then). The phone **rings** (now); the phone **rang** (then). As you edit or proofread for the right verb forms, ask yourself:

■ Are things happening now—in the **present?** The plain or unmarked form of verbs show that the time is now. (Many customers now **order** products by e-mail. They **pay** by credit card.) Read the examples over several times:

NORMAL PRESENT: Agents **check** tickets. Trains **leave** all day. They **live** in the suburbs.
                    Drivers **stop** for pedestrians. Youngsters **go** to school.

In many sentences, however, we change the plain or unmarked form while we still stay in the present. When we talk about a single third party (or a single object or idea), we add the -*s* ending. (E-mail now **makes** regular mail unnecessary. A careful customer **pays** attention to the fine print.)

THIRD PERSON ONLY: The agents **checks** your ticket. The train **leaves** at eight. Simon **lives** at home.
                       The bus **stops** here. The music **goes** on and on.

■ Are you reporting things that happened in the **past?** Change your verbs to forms that show past. (The accident **happened** quickly. The guard **locked** us out.)

PAST: The agent **checked** our ticket. The train **left** on time. His parents **lived** in the country.
          The bus **stopped** and **went** on.

English has two different ways of showing action in the past. The most common is the added -*d* or -*ed* ending. Check your writing for this missing ending. Read the examples over several times:

-*ed* ENDING: At the beginning of the term, we **registered, signed** up for courses, **checked** out the
                  parking, **started** conversations, **complained** about the lines, and **investigated** campus
                  hangouts.
-*ed* ENDING: Developers **designed** new malls, **constructed** apartment buildings, **opened** new
                  stores, **pushed** ahead with ambitious plans, **changed** zoning laws, and **appealed** to
                  the voters.

The second way of showing action in the past is to change the whole word: **think** (now)/**thought** (then); **write** (now)/**wrote** (then); **drive** (now)/**drove** (then); **choose** (now)/**chose** (then); **lose** (now)/**lost** (then).

UNUSUAL PAST: At the end of the term, we **felt** the pressure, **wrote** term papers, **took** our final
                  exams, **went** to commencement, and **drove** home.

185

- Are you talking about the more **distant past?** If necessary, show that something had happened earlier—*before* other events in the past. For most English verbs, use the *-ed* form when you go back into the more distant past. Use it whenever your main verb comes after *have, has,* or *had:* **have called, has called, had called.** Read the examples over several times:

DISTANT PAST: Nobody **had called.** The voters **had approved** the plans. The court **had overturned** the conviction. The governor **had vetoed** the law. She **had married** a second cousin. The police **would have towed** the car.

Use the same *-ed* form when you use *have* or *has* to look back from the *present* at something in the past that is still true or still important:

STILL TRUE: The relatives disapprove, but she **has married** her second cousin.
Racism still exists, but attitudes **have changed.**

The same unusual verbs that don't use the *-ed* ending for the past also use unusual forms for the more distant past. Sometimes you have to know only two forms: **lose** (now), **lost** (past), **had lost** (distant past). Sometimes you have to know three forms: **write** (now), **wrote** (past), **had written** (distant past). Read the examples over several times:

DISTANT PAST: Nobody **had written.** The plans **had fallen** apart. The judges **had chosen** a winner. The chef **had gone** home. She **had** never **driven** that far. Your friends **might have lost** their way.

- Are you talking about something **being done?** Use the same forms you used after *have (has, had).* Use them after the many forms of *be (am, is, are, was, were, has been)* when you talk about something being done (**passive**). Again, check especially for the *-ed* ending. Read the examples over several times:

PASSIVE: Endangered species **are protected** by law. The contract **was terminated.** The workers **were rehired.** The conviction **has been overturned.** The project **should** never **have been approved.** The plan **will be revised.**

- **IMPORTANT EXCEPTION:**   Use the plain or unmarked form (and not the *-ed* form) with *do, does,* or *did.* We use forms of *do* to make up **questions** (**Did** you **notify** the police?). We use them also to make up negative statements—statements that say no (We **do not accept** credit cards).

QUESTIONS: Why **did** the police **suspect** the janitor? (NOT: *suspected*)
Did the package **arrive** on time? (NOT: *arrived*)
How **did** the prisoner **escape?** (NOT: *escaped*)
NEGATIVE: The agent **did** not **confirm** the date. (NOT: *confirmed*)

INSTANT REVIEW

Put a check mark for each sentence that has the right form of the verb.

1   Sports were once segregated by race. _____
2   White and black audiences attend separate games. _____
3   Now the sports fan support winners of any race. _____
4   Sports like basketball are now dominated by minority athletes. _____
5   Tennis audiences had expect white contenders. _____
6   Football teams had hired few minority coaches. _____
7   Over the years, attitudes changed. _____
8   Women's sports have made great strides. _____
9   In 1999, the Women's World Cup attract 90,000 spectators. _____
10   No women's event had ever been watched by that many. _____

Name _____

EDITING PRACTICE
    Enter the right forms in the blank spaces.

America's Unwanted

    The melting pot has often been (use) _____ to describe the diverse racial make-up

that now (constitute) _____ the American population. The editor of *American Heritage*

has (write) _____ that it is here in America where "(individual) _____

of all (nation) _____ are (melt) _____ into a new race" of (citizen)

_____. Old World nations had (emphasize) _____ the many (difference)

_____ that have always (distinguish) _____ them from other (country)

_____. Here the original (inhabitant) _____ or the early (settler)

_____ are considered no more American than later (arrival) _____. We are

a nation of foreigners who are (link) _____ by the common thread of immigration.

    Although Americans have often (claim) _____ to be a (nation)

_____ of immigrants, we have not always (extend) _____ open arms

to the newcomers. Today's historians (acknowledge) _____ that Americans have often

(feel) _____ animosity toward immigrant groups. Politicians a few years ago (exploit)

_____ a backlash against "aliens," but an earlier generation had (work)

_____ the same side of the street.

    Earlier waves of immigrants did not always (encounter) _____ a warm welcome.

Anti-immigrant feelings (mount) _____ in the 1840s and (focus) _____

especially on the Irish. Although the Irish were (discriminate) _____ against because they were Catholic, the English Protestants (use) _____ the poor Irish economic situation as an

excuse to deny them entry into America. Today Irish Americans (excel) _____ everywhere

in American politics, business, and education, and an Irish American president is (remember)

_____ as one of America's most beloved (leader) _____.

As time passed, society (redirect) _____ its social prejudices away from the Irish

and on to other cultures. During World War II, many Japanese were (place) _____ in

internment camps and (deprive) _____ of their property and liberty. One elderly (woman)

_____ who had been (intern) _____ in one of these (camp)

_____ described the situation to me by saying: "Not only did they (make)

_____ me feel like less than a citizen, they (make) _____ me feel

like less than a human being."

Today prejudice in America often (target) _____ the Latin American population.

Mexican American immigrants have been (blame) _____ for taking jobs away or for

abusing welfare or public (service) _____. When he was governor of California, a leading

Republican politician (support) _____ a movement to deny health care and schooling to

(child) _____ of undocumented immigrants from Mexico. Many in the immigrant

community felt they were (give) _____ a bad rap and (use) _____

as scapegoats for the governor's inability to govern effectively. If America constantly (portray)

_____ itself as the land of opportunity, why not allow immigrants the chance to

partake in this great American illusion?

INDEX

Notes to Readers: Boldfaced numbers direct you to the unit numbers in the workbook. Unit numbers preceded by **(std)** direct you to Units 31–32 on standard English. Unit numbers preceded by **(esl)** direct you to Units 44–47 on English as a second language.